HOLY COMMUNION

Latimer Monographs

Latimer Papers

LATIMER MONOGRAPHS
III

THE SERVICE OF

HOLY
COMMUNION

AND ITS

REVISION

EDITED BY

R. T. Beckwith

*(Librarian, Latimer House, and Visiting Lecturer on Liturgy,
Wycliffe College, Oxford)*

WITH

J. E. Tiller

(Lecturer on Liturgy, Trinity College, Bristol)

THE MARCHAM MANOR PRESS
APPLEFORD   ABINGDON   BERKSHIRE

LATIMER HOUSE, OXFORD

LATIMER House, Oxford, is a centre for study and research. It is committed to the ideal of creatively applying biblical and Reformation theology to the ongoing life of the Church of England and the Anglican Communion.

Latimer Monographs are a series of occasional studies on doctrinal and liturgical subjects which bear on issues of importance for Anglicans today. They are written by members of the Anglican Communion who share the standpoint of Latimer House.

JOHN STOTT, *Chairman of Council*
JOHN WENHAM, *Warden*

Set in eleven point monotype **Baskerville**
two point leaded

Printed in Great Britain by Stanley L. Hunt (Printers) Ltd., Rushden

CONTENTS

To John Stafford Wright
under whom the Editors studied and afterwards taught
They dedicate this token
of their gratitude, affection and respect

ACKNOWLEDGMENTS

Grateful acknowledgments are made to Church in Wales Publications for permission to quote from *Tell Wales* and from *The Liturgical Congress at Carmarthen*; to the Church of England Liturgical Commission for permission to quote from *Liturgical Reform: Some Basic Principles*; and to the Church Literature Association for permission to quote from A. H. Couratin's *Lambeth and Liturgy*.

Preface

THIS MONOGRAPH IS a sequel to Latimer Monograph 2:
Services of Baptism and Confirmation (Marcham Manor Press,
1967). Like its predecessor, it is not designed to encourage
unauthorised experimentation, but to influence the future
course of official Prayer Book revision, whether or not the
service it contains can be authorised for experimental use under
the Alternative Services Measure. It is also designed to help
people to assess the Liturgical Commission's Series 3 service,
when deciding in what form the General Synod should authorise
it, or whether a parish should use it.

The service contained in this monograph was drawn up by
the Liturgy Group centred at Latimer House, Oxford, though
the final responsibility for it rests with the two editors. Not
all members of the Group listed at the end of this preface have
been active during the whole period of the preparation of the
service, and there are a few features of the service to which not
all members are equally committed. Nevertheless, it has the
general support of the whole Group, who would envisage it
being used with allowance for the 'variations which are not
of substantial importance' permitted by the Alternative Services
Measure. In the course of the preparation of the service, drafts
have been submitted to the Federation of Diocesan Evangelical
Unions, to a number of its constituent Unions, to the national
conference of the Eclectic Society (a society consisting of
several hundreds of younger Evangelical Anglican clergy), and

to many individual scholars, pastors and legislators, including a considerable number of members of the House of Laity. Their response has, on the whole, been most encouraging, and their criticisms have led to many improvements, for which we owe them our sincere thanks. Expert linguistic criticisms have been made by Arthur Pollard, Professor of English at Hull University, and by the Rev. A. C. Thiselton. To them also we express our thanks.

The introductory chapters are the work of the editors, who alone must be held responsible for them, though the editors are deeply indebted to their discussions with the other members of the Liturgy Group over many years. The Liturgy Group, which includes parochial clergy, clergy in academic work, one layman, several members of the old Church Assembly and the new General Synod, and one member of the Church of England Liturgical Commission, first turned its attention to the Holy Communion service in 1962, when it began to comment on the early drafts of *A Liturgy for Africa* (London, SPCK, 1964).[1] At the beginning of 1965 it started to prepare for a revision of its own, the firstfruits of which work was *A Eucharist for the Seventies*, by C. H. B. Byworth and B. T. Lloyd (1968, now distributed by Grove Books, Bramcote, Nottingham).[2] This was one of two radical revisions of the Communion service which different members of the Group drew up from first principles, but in the meantime the Church of England Liturgical Commission had published its own radical revision at the end of 1965, in *Alternative Services: Second Series* (London, SPCK),[3] and the interest and controversy which this notable service aroused turned the attention of the Group to the task of trying to make it more biblical and edifying. The improvements which were made or called for by Church Assembly before the service was authorised for experimental use, and the further improvements which have now been made by the Liturgical Commission in the *Third Series* version, do not seem to the Group to have rendered their work at all superfluous. With all its merits, the service still has quite a long way to go

8

before it can qualify as a permanent part of Anglican worship, and the hope expressed by the chairman of the Liturgical Commission that Series 3 may be regarded as definitive and may be incorporated in a new Prayer Book by about 1975-6 (*A Commentary on Holy Communion Series* 3, London, SPCK, 1971, p.3) is unfortunately premature.

Alongside their work on the Liturgical Commission's service, the Group began work on a recognisable revision of the 1662 service. Since the Liturgical Commission evidently had no interest in such a task, and *Holy Communion: First Series* was disqualified from filling such a role by its doctrinal characteristics and its antiquated language, it fell wholly to an unofficial group like ours to see what could be done to bring 1662 into the twentieth century. Already the comparison between the Prayer Book service and the Liturgical Commission's service during the experimental period was being hopelessly distorted by the unequal terms of the comparison between a twentieth century service and one three hundred years old, and it was possible to foresee that at the end of the experimental period those who might not wish to use the new service for doctrinal reasons would be treated in the same way as Evangelicals have been treated in the Scottish Episcopal Church and the Church of the Province of South Africa, and would be told that they were graciously permitted to use the unaltered 1662 service instead. The reward of doctrinal faithfulness, in those circumstances, is to be branded with the image of living in the past. Of course, many Evangelicals are already using the Liturgical Commission's service, in the confidence that its doctrinal blemishes and deficiencies will be remedied before it reaches its final form, but they too would doubtless welcome as an alternative an updating of the 1662 service, which has such a warm place in an Evangelical's affections. The experimental revision of the Communion service recently produced in South Africa suggested the possibility of merging the chief characteristics of the Antecommunion of the Series 2-3 and 1662 services, and producing a single order of Ante-

9

communion followed by alternative orders of Communion, and this is what we have done.[4] One may add, that if it became clear that a modernised 1662 had a secure place in the future worship of the Church of England, it would be quite possible to agree to the alternative orders of Communion being made a good deal more different than we have made them at present, by the omission from Series 2-3 Revised of most of the items derived from 1662 which the Liturgical Commission did not venture to omit or Church Assembly required them to restore, and which we have left as purely optional. It would probably not be desirable, however, to omit any item which is here made obligatory. Nor would it be desirable to introduce small differences between closely similar items which have here been made textually identical (following either 1662 or Series 2-3, whichever seemed best), since small differences of this kind confuse the worshipper.

In drawing up these services, the Liturgy Group has profited from its acquaintanceship with earlier revisions drawn up by Evangelicals, particularly *A Liturgical Essay*, by Albert Mitchell, *An Evangelical Eucharist*, by the Rev. L. E. H. Stephens-Hodge, and *A Modern Liturgy*, drafted for the Prayer Book Commission of the Church of England in Australia by Canon D. W. B. Robinson.[5] The Group also owes debts, of course, to other liturgies and writings on liturgy, ancient and modern, emanating from outside the Evangelical school. In particular, their debt to Series 2-3 (and its ancient sources) is pervasive.[6] Among their alternatives to the Ten Commandments, our Lord's Summary derives ultimately from the Non-Jurors' Liturgy of 1718,[7] and the Beatitudes from Jeremy Taylor's liturgy and the 1689 proposals for the comprehension of Nonconformists.[8] Their form for the dismissal derives from a biblical source, Ruth 2. 4. It is to the Bible, together with the Prayer Book, that their chief debt is owed.

The members of the Liturgy Group during the period since 1965 are the two editors, together with A. Bennett, D. D. Billings, A. J. Bishop, C. O. Buchanan, C. H. B. Byworth,

P. S. Dawes, G. E. Duffield, C. H. Hutchins, B. T. Lloyd, G. Ogilvie, D. M. Paterson, J. A. Simpson, J. T. Tabor, and C. Wyatt.

Notes

1. The reflections of the Liturgy Group on this service formed the basis for the articles 'Lambeth 1958 and the Liturgy for Africa', by R. T. Beckwith, in *The Churchman*, vol. 79, no. 4 (December 1965); vol. 80, no. 1 (March 1966).

2. This has attracted some favourable comment. The commendations by Catholic Anglicans such as A. B. Wilkinson (in *Faith and Unity*, vol. 13, no. 5, September 1969) have been particularly gratifying.

3. Assessments of the *Alternative Services* by Liturgy Group members and others associated with them were published in *Towards a Modern Prayer Book*, ed. R. T. Beckwith (Marcham Manor Press, 1966); in an article by J. A. Simpson, 'The New Alternative Services', in *The Churchman*, vol. 80, no. 1 (March 1966); in *The New Communion Service: Reasons for Dissent* and *A Guide to Second Series Communion Service*, by C. O. Buchanan (London, Church Book Room Press, 1966); and in *The Second Series Communion Service: What are the Issues?* by R. T. Beckwith (London, Church Book Room Press, 1969).

4. See *Proposed Alternative Forms of Morning and Evening Prayer and Holy Communion* (Cape Town, Liturgical Committee of the Church of the Province of South Africa, 1969).

5. An account of these three revisions is given at the end of chapter one. Mr. Stephens-Hodge was for a short time a member of the Latimer House Liturgy Group.

6. Some account of the sources of Series 2-3 is given in H. de Candole and A. H. Couratin, *Re-Shaping the Liturgy* (London, CIO for Liturgical Commission, 1964). It may be added that the broadening of the Prayer for the Church to include the world goes back, via the Ceylon Liturgy, to three of the liturgies included in W. J. Grisbrooke, *Anglican Liturgies of the Seventeenth and Eighteenth Centuries* (London, SPCK for Alcuin Club, 1958), and has ancient precedents in the *Apostolic Constitutions* and the supposed early intercessions of the Roman liturgy (see G. G. Willis, *Essays in Early Roman Liturgy*, London, SPCK for Alcuin

Club, 1964, ch. 1).   An intercession of corresponding scope has been restored in the Roman Antecommunion since Vatican II.
7. Reprinted in Grisbrooke.   On our Lord's Summary, see ' "These Two Commandments" in Liturgy and Catechism,' by C. L. Berry, in the *Modern Churchman*, vol. 8, no. 3 (April 1965).
8. The former is reprinted in Grisbrooke. The latter was reprinted in the last century as *The Revised Liturgy of 1689*, ed. John Taylor (London, Bagster, 1855).

1 The Background to Revision

THOUGH REVISION OF the Church's liturgy has gone on intermittently throughout Christian history, it received a unique stimulus at the Reformation, when all the customs and traditions of the Church were called in question, and the attempt was made, in an earnest and thorough way, to test and reform them by the Bible. The manner in which the English Reformers pursued this aim in relation to the liturgy is described in the Prayer Book, especially in the two prefatory statements 'Concerning the Service of the Church' and 'Of Ceremonies'. They attempted to attain intelligibility, edification and corporateness, by the use of a single, simple liturgy in the vernacular, in which the Scriptures were read in an orderly way, biblical teaching was incorporated throughout, all that was meaningless or misleading was excluded, and congregational participation in speaking, singing and reception of the sacrament (in both kinds) was encouraged. In pursuing these goals, there were limits to what the Reformers could achieve. No doubt, like all other students of the Bible, they had their blind spots, though fewer than is often alleged today. Also, confronted with a largely illiterate Church, and long-standing habits of infrequent lay communion, it was not possible to follow their aim of congregational worship as far as would have been ideal. Another effect of illiteracy (and of political needs) was that it necessitated carrying simplicity and uniformity to lengths which greatly restricted variety and freedom. Never-

theless, the Anglican reformation of worship was an extra-
ordinary achievement, and its success was much assisted by
the twin factors of Cranmer's liturgical genius and his policy
of trying to begin from where people were, by taking as his
starting point the existing practice of the Church, and not
substituting anything fresh except where edification seemed to
him, in the current circumstances of the nation, to require it.

Cranmer had a great respect for antiquity, and especially
for the writings of the early Fathers, who stood nearest to the
New Testament in point of time, and had been least affected
by later deviations from its teaching. The Prayer Book states
that he took various hints from the Fathers when revising the
liturgy. His criterion for judging the Fathers, however, was
the same as his criterion for judging everything else, namely
Scripture. As chapters 2 and 7 of his *Confutation of Unwritten
Verities* clearly show, he refused to treat their writings as a
norm, and recognised faults in them which were not to be
imitated. For this reason, therefore, added to his conservative
attitude towards existing practice, he made no attempt to
restore patristic worship except where change was necessary
for the sake of edification, and patristic worship supplied the
best available model. The idea recently current that Cranmer's chief aim in producing the Prayer Book was to restore
ancient liturgical practice, and that the chief obstacle in his
path was his ignorance of what ancient liturgical practice was
like, is false on both counts. This was demonstrated at some
length in Latimer Monograph 2 (pp. 27-30), and what was
said there does not need to be repeated here. Cranmer's
policy towards antiquity was essentially selective, and no other
policy is implied in the 1559, 1604 or 1662 revisions of his
Prayer Book, as is clear from the contemporary evidence of
the 1604 Canons (Canons 30-33, 42, 60, 74, 91), from the 1662
'Preface', and from the fact that, despite increasing knowledge
of ancient worship, his Prayer Book was retained, in each of
these three revisions, essentially unchanged.

During the seventeenth century, however, antiquity began

to be cultivated by certain scholars for its own sake. The first result in the field of Prayer Book revision was the Scottish Communion service of 1637, in which the consecration prayer, like that of Cranmer's first Communion service of 1549, concluded with the Prayer of Oblation and the Lord's Prayer. The attraction of this order was that in fourth century liturgies the *anamnesis* (which consists of words of commemoration and oblation) and the Lord's Prayer often come in similar positions. The process of restoring fourth century practice was carried a good deal further by the Usager Nonjurors, who had broken with the Church of England, by their successors among the Scottish and American Episcopalians, and by certain eccentric individuals inside and outside the Church of England, such as Edward Stephens, William Whiston and Orator Henley. Whiston and Henley found their Arian views supported by the fourth century *Apostolic Constitutions*, which they believed to be the genuine work of the apostles; they were therefore eager for the restoration of the liturgy which the *Constitutions* contain. An exaggerated idea of the antiquity of pre-Reformation liturgies was common among such enthusiasts, and even in the nineteenth century the leading Anglo-Catholic liturgiologist J. M. Neale held that the Liturgy of St. Mark might safely be attributed to the evangelist Mark and his immediate followers, that the liturgy in the *Apostolic Constitutions* was in all main points the liturgy taught by St. Paul to the churches of his foundation, and that the Liturgy of St. James was written by someone present at the Last Supper and Pentecost, and is quoted in 1 Cor. 2. 9.[1] It is now agreed among scholars that none of these liturgies is as old as the *Apostolic Tradition* of Hippolytus, which itself dates only from the early third century; and though *The Search for an Apostolic Liturgy*, as R. C. D. Jasper calls it in the title of his little record of the quest (London, Mowbray for Alcuin Club, 1963), has continued to beguile such great figures in the liturgical world as W. H. Frere, a strong body of liturgical opinion has now developed which maintains that the further back one goes in liturgical history, the greater the diversity and fluidity that one discovers; and that those resemblances between the extant liturgies which cannot be traced to the New Testament or Judaism are probably due not to a common origin in the apostolic age, but to the influence of one liturgy upon another at a relatively late date.[2]

The enthusiasts for antiquity among revisers of the Prayer Book have had as their contemporaries revisers of quite other kinds. In the volumes of Peter Hall's *Reliquiae Liturgicae* and *Fragmenta Liturgica* (Bath, Binns and Goodwin, 1847, 1848), from which W. J. Grisbrooke has made the decidedly tendentious selection printed in his *Anglican Liturgies of the Seventeenth and Eighteenth Centuries*, there are Puritan and Arian revisions which show no interest in antiquity at all. The same lack of interest in antiquity characterises many of the nineteenth century revisions described in A. E. Peaston's book *The Prayer Book Revisions of the Victorian Evangelicals* (Dublin, APCK, 1963). When one adds these revisions to the strongly Cranmerian revisions adopted by the Church of England in 1604 and 1662, and by the Church of Ireland in 1878, it can be seen that in the seventeenth, eighteenth and nineteenth centuries the course of Prayer Book revision was by no means running in one direction only. That it has tended to run only in one direction during the twentieth century must be attributed to the power of the Oxford Movement, and to the lead that the heirs of the Oxford Movement have taken in Anglican liturgical studies. The collection of eucharistic liturgies from Anglican Churches abroad made by Bernard Wigan under the title *The Liturgy in English* (2nd ed., London, OUP, 1964) shows clearly how much the influence of pre-Reformation liturgy has recently been at work. Only in the first Canadian Prayer Book of 1918 and the second Irish Prayer Book of 1926 is Cranmer the predominant influence. The still more recent experimental liturgies collected by C. O. Buchanan in his work *Modern Anglican Liturgies 1958-1968* (London, OUP, 1968) show the ideals of the Oxford Movement still paramount in most cases, though not in all.

The Oxford Movement was a new departure in Anglican history, inasmuch as it was concerned to restore not just pre-Reformation practice but pre-Reformation doctrine. It can never be repeated too often that the lovers of antiquity among seventeenth century Anglican divines were on the whole firmly Protestant in their theology, and not least in their eucharistic theology. Even the Usager Nonjurors had no great love of unreformed theology, which is why their negotiations with the Eastern Orthodox so speedily came to grief. The material sacrifice in the eucharist which they asserted was a sacrifice of bread and wine. The real presence which they affirmed was an impanation (a localisation in bread) of the Holy Spirit. Their opinions were therefore eccentric rather than unreformed, and were very far from qualifying as Catholic orthodoxy.[3] Where unreformed theology is well known to be rejected, it is not impracticable, for those who so desire, to restore forms of worship which were not actually designed to exclude such theology, and which history has shown to lend themselves to it. But if there is a definite wish to restore unreformed theology, the impulse to restore such forms of worship, as its expression, becomes imperative, and features of them will be restored which in other circumstances would have been deliberately left behind. Hence the trend of Prayer Book revision in the twentieth century, building on foundations which had been unwittingly laid for it in earlier centuries.[4]

Along with the attempt to restore pre-Reformation doctrine and worship, the Oxford Movement also gave birth to an attempt to reinterpret Anglican history, so as to justify what was being restored, by showing it to be less novel than was supposed. Here again the lovers of antiquity in the seventeenth and eighteenth centuries gave the Tractarians some unintentional help. The Laudian historian Peter Heylyn, for example, had maintained in his *Ecclesia Restaurata, or the History of the Reformation of the Church of England* (1661) that the first Prayer Book of Edward VI expressed the true mind of the English Reformers, and that the changes in the second were

17

made because of pressure from the Arminians' great bugbear Calvin. To an Anglo-Catholic like Bishop Frere, however, the difference between the two Prayer Books is not just one of traditional practice but of doctrine: the 1549 Prayer Book left the doctrine of the real presence in the elements untouched, whereas the 1552 Prayer Book excluded it.[5] Similarly, it has been common for Anglo-Catholic liturgiologists to maintain that the history of the Prayer Book from 1559 to 1662 (when the Laudians Cosin and Wren dominated the work of revision) was a quiet restoration not just of certain liturgical features of the 1549 Book, but of the Catholic doctrine of that Book, which subsequent developments have only made explicit, not introduced *de novo*. But on these points also opinion among liturgiologists is changing. It was only to be expected that Evangelical liturgiologists, such as J. C. Robertson, William Goode, J. T. Tomlinson, Nathaniel Dimock and T. W. Drury, would not be prepared to accept the proposed reinterpretation of history. But they have since found allies in a variety of quarters. As early as 1890 two Roman Catholics, the historian F. A. Gasquet and the liturgiologist Edmund Bishop, collaborated to produce *Edward VI and the Book of Common Prayer: an Examination into its Origin and Early History with an Appendix of Unpublished Documents* (London, Hodges). They here drew attention to the Protestant influences on Cranmer's first Prayer Book (not just his second); to the record of the 1548 debate in parliament on the first Prayer Book, in which the Reforming bishops are already expressing their mature Protestant views on the eucharist; to the letter written from Lambeth by Bucer and Fagius on 26 April 1549, just before the 1549 Prayer Book came into use, stating that it is only intended as an interim measure; and to Cranmer and Gardiner's literary controversy on the eucharist between the appearance of the two Prayer Books, in which Cranmer refuses to admit the legitimacy of any of Gardiner's appeals to the 1549 Book in favour of unreformed doctrine, maintaining that it is intended to express the views that he now holds and nothing else. In our own generation, certain distinguished Anglo-Catholic liturgiologists, Gregory Dix, E. C. Ratcliff and A. H. Couratin, have shown a distinct tendency to adopt similar views. Dix, for example, held that the 1552 Communion service is not a falling away from the 1549 service, but is Cranmer's masterpiece, expressing the same beliefs and aims in a more clear and consistent way.

> It is *not* a disordered attempt at a catholic rite, but the only effective attempt ever made to give liturgical expression to the doctrine of 'justification by faith alone' (*The Shape of the Liturgy*, London, Dacre Press, 1945, p. 672).

Couratin is equally clear that the 1549 Book expresses Cranmer's mature eucharistic views (*The Service of Holy Communion 1549-1662*, London, SPCK, 1963, pp. 3-5, 8-12), and holds that 'the rite of 1552 is a superb piece of liturgical composition, the finest flower of Reformation liturgy'.[6] Passing on to the 1637 and 1662 Communion services, Ratcliff declared that

> For all their patristic interest the Anglican divines of the seventeenth century never abandoned a reformed position as to the effects of consecration. Their Eucharistic doctrine was mostly Calvinist; and they firmly held to the idea of the permanence of the substances of the bread and wine.[7]

Finally, a liturgiologist of a different school again, G. J. Cuming, has recently discredited the long-standing belief that the predominant influence in the preparation of the 1662 Prayer Book was that of the Laudians Cosin and Wren (strongly Protestant as they in many respects were). The Laudians, Cuming shows, despite their hard work, were overruled on all the most controversial matters. The real influence lay with much more moderate men, notably Sanderson, who were closely in touch with the intensely conservative mood of Convocation and Parliament, where all suggestions for radical change, whether Laudian or Puritan, were resisted.[8]

Since the restoration of patristic worship was not one of the foundation principles of Anglicanism, since those who are ardent to restore it have never been more than one school of thought among Anglicans, since the idea that patristic worship is apostolic has proved delusive, and since, where restored, it has brought with it those unreformed doctrines from which the earlier enthusiasts for antiquity were anxious to dissociate it, it might seem that the obvious course for Anglicans today is to make a break with current liturgical trends, and to return to the liturgical principles of Cranmer. This, we believe, is indeed going to happen, and the 'Liturgical Movement', with its stress on simplicity, intelligibility and corporateness, is a long step in the right direction. But the change of policy will not be carried out thoroughly and consistently until earlier trends have fully spent their force. Catholic Anglicans still lead the way in liturgical studies, and though the historical case for Anglo-Catholicism is in disarray, the doctrinal case has not as yet been overthrown or abandoned, at any rate in the realm of the sacraments. However, a few years may bring dramatic changes here also. This is partly because Roman theology, on which Anglo-Catholicism has so greatly depended, is losing its stability and moving in unwonted directions; and partly because the experiment of producing the book *Growing into Union* (London, SPCK, 1970) suggests that Anglo-Catholics and Evangelicals can, if they try, make real headway in sorting out their theological differences. In the meantime, a return to Cranmer's liturgical principles has been hindered by the claim that the 1662 Prayer Book should no longer be regarded as the norm of doctrine or worship for the Anglican Communion. This proposal was first put forward by the Church of England Liturgical Commission in its report *Prayer Book Revision in the Church of England* (London, SPCK, 1957, pp. 35-38), and was taken up by the subcommittee on the Book of Common Prayer at the 1958 Lambeth Conference (*The Lambeth Conference 1958*, London, SPCK, 1958, pp. 2:78-81 and Resolution 74c), of which the then chairman of the Liturgical Commission was a leading member.[9] The plea on which the proposal was based was that the right norm for Anglican Liturgy is the worship of the primitive Church, at which

Cranmer himself was aiming. It is entirely understandable that the Liturgical Commission should have made this proposal (dubious as its grounds are), since the most influential member of the Commission in 1957 was the late E. C. Ratcliff, who (like his disciple A. H. Couratin, also on the Commission) had come to the conclusion that the Book of Common Prayer was an essentially Protestant production. He doubtless inferred that the best hope of establishing Catholic principles lay not in rearranging the parts of the Prayer Book service, which had been the basic method with Anglo-Catholic revisers up to that time,[10] but in making a clean break with the Prayer Book and beginning anew. Whether, in certain circumstances, there are other and better reasons for drawing up a fresh service from first principles will be discussed in chapter four. The point to notice here is that the radical revision which the Liturgical Commission subsequently produced has aroused precisely the same doctrinal controversies as the earlier attempts to catholicise Cranmer. It had to be modified in order to get it authorised, and in its resultant form some Evangelicals find it too Catholic to be tolerable, and some Anglo-Catholics find it equally intolerable because it is not Catholic enough.[11] The changes made in the *Third Series* version seem likely to harden Anglo-Catholic opposition, while not removing all grounds for opposition by Evangelicals. Until serious account is taken of the fact that theological objections can only be satisfied by theological reasoning, no improvement in this situation can be expected.

Ever since the early years of this century, the policy which has governed the Church of England has been one of attempting to restore order and discipline by making theological and liturgical concessions to Anglo-Catholicism and Liberalism, and then asking people to be satisfied and to conform.[12] The Liturgical Commission's service is a further example of this policy. Order and discipline are a worthy aim: the Church of England today has too little of either. But one cannot restore them by a policy of appeasement, which never asks questions of truth. In face of this policy, the traditional Evangelical resistance to doctrinal and liturgical change has been understandable and right, and so has the Anglo-Catholic refusal to be satisfied with limited concessions. Nothing will break the deadlock, short of the achievement of a real theological understanding and consensus (if such proves possible) between the contending parties. At the present juncture, the Church of England would be wiser to spend its money on commissions concerned with this, rather than on commissions appointed to talk to other denominations.

But if such a consensus were reached (it may be asked), would Evangelicals want Prayer Book revision any more than before? The answer is an emphatic yes, and this book may be regarded as an earnest of the fact.

Evangelicals have never been opposed to Prayer Book revision altogether. One or two innocent souls may doubtless be found who see no need for change, but Evangelicals in general are fully aware that a seventeenth century book is not adequate for twentieth century needs. Even in 1927-28 it was admitted by the fairest and best informed critics of the Evangelicals that they were prepared for a revision of the Irish type, in which there were no doctrinal innovations and there were *seen* to be none; and it was only when they were presented with the choice of a revision of another type or none at all that they opted for none at all. In the preparations for the 1928 book the leading Evangelical liturgiologist, Bishop Drury, was extremely active, and as late as 1921 the Church Assembly had before it an anamnesis which was essentially the joint work of Drury and Frere. It was only after Drury's death that the consecration prayer assumed the controversial (and grotesque) form that it has in the 1928 book.

Drury's mantle fell upon the less learned but not undistinguished shoulders of Albert Mitchell, who was not in a position of such influence and had a very difficult part to play. Nevertheless, he was so far from being opposed to all revision that he drew up a communion service as a positive alternative to the official proposals, which, with westward position, an Old Testament lesson added to the epistle and gospel, a psalm and canticle between the lessons, and new provisions for supplementary consecration, was far more forward-looking than many revisions produced by people of other schools of thought decades later.[13]

More recent Evangelical ventures in the field of eucharistic revision have included L. E. H. Stephens-Hodge's *Evangelical Eucharist*, which made the interesting experiment of linking the offertory of alms with the Prayer of Oblation after communion, thus reviving the position for the offertory of alms attested by Justin Martyr (*First Apology*, ch. 67) and the third century *Didascalia* (ch. 9) and desired by Bishop Hooper (*Early Writings*, Parker Society, p. 537);[14] and D. W. B. Robinson's *Modern Liturgy* (in *Prayer Book Revision in Australia*, Sydney, Standing Committee of the General Synod, 1966), which was one of the first two revisions in modern English, and is remarkable both in locating the Lord's Prayer with the intercession, and in having separate thanksgivings over the bread and the wine, with permission for separate administration after each. Today, it is true to say that wherever in the Anglican Communion Prayer Book revision is under discussion, there Evangelicals are taking an active interest in it. In C. O. Buchanan's *Modern Anglican Liturgies 1958-1968*, Evangelical contributors from fourteen different areas of the Anglican Communion describe and interpret liturgical developments in their own area. And though in some places there may be little that Evangelicals can do beyond putting a check on other schools of thought, Australia is not the only country where Evangelicals are under no such pressure and are ready to take an initiative.

Notes

1. *The Liturgies of S. Mark, S. James, S. Clement, S. Chrysostom, S. Basil* (4th ed., London, Dickinson, 1896), pp. 3, 37, 79, 83f.
2. See, for example, J. H. Srawley, *The Early History of the Liturgy* (2nd ed., Cambridge, The University Press, 1947), pp. xi-xiii; E. C. Ratcliff, 'The Shape of the Liturgy', in *Theology*, vol. 48, no. 300 (June 1945), p. 128.
3. See C. S. Carter, *The Anglican 'Via Media', being studies in the Elizabethan Religious Settlement and the Teaching of the Caroline Divines* (London, Thynne and Jarvis, 1927); R. T. Beckwith,

Priesthood and Sacraments (Latimer Monograph 1, Marcham Manor Press, 1964), ch. 5. See also the quotation from E. C. Ratcliff a little later in this chapter, and W. J. Grisbrooke, *op. cit.*, where the commentary on the texts is clear and frank about their theological background.

4. As M. H. Shepherd Jr., himself an American Anglican, put it in his address to the Minneapolis Anglican Congress, the sacrificial consecration prayers of the Scottish and American liturgies so prepared the way that it has since been 'possible to reintroduce once more the whole scholastic theology of the Eucharist against which the Reformers rebelled. That this position has been taken by many Anglicans within the last century cannot be denied' ('Our Anglican Understanding of Corporate Worship', in *Report of the Anglican Congress 1954*, London, SPCK, 1955, p. 81f.).

5. See F. Procter and W. H. Frere, *A New History of the Book of Common Prayer* (3rd impression, London, Macmillan, 1941), p. 82f.

6. 'The Eucharist under Revision,' in *Tell Wales* (Penarth, Church in Wales Publications, 1964), p. 41. Elsewhere, Couratin speaks of the 'unimpeachably Protestant character' of the Book of Common Prayer ('Liturgy', in *The Pelican Guide to Modern Theology*, ed. R. P. C. Hanson, Harmondsworth, Penguin Books, 1969-1970, vol. 2, p. 232).

7. 'Christian Worship and Liturgy,' in *The Study of Theology*, ed. K. E. Kirk (London, Hodder and Stoughton, 1939), p. 463. Compare also what he says of the background of the Scottish liturgy of 1764 on p. 465f.

8. 'The Making of the Prayer Book of 1662,' in A. M. Ramsey and others, *The English Prayer Book 1549-1662* (London, SPCK, 1963); *A History of Anglican Liturgy* (London, Macmillan, 1969), ch. 7.

9. There is a full discussion of this proposal in the first instalment of the article 'Lambeth 1958 and the Liturgy for Africa', by R. T. Beckwith, in *The Churchman*, vol. 79, no. 4 (December 1965).

10. Many of the texts in *The Liturgy in English*, ed. B. J. Wigan, demonstrate this, and *Holy Communion: First Series* (which was forced through Church Assembly against strenuous Evangelical resistance) is a recent example. As noted earlier, the method was taken over from the Carolines and their successors. Its history has been traced in 'Alternative Services: the Canon of Series 1', by J. M. M. Dalby, in the *Church Quarterly Review*, vol. 168, no. 369 (October 1967).

11. For able expressions of these two points of view, see D. A.

Scales, *What Mean ye by this Service?* (Cambridge, Truth and Faith
Committee, 1969), and G. G. Willis, *1966 and All That* (London,
League of Anglican Loyalists, 1969).

12. See *Prayer Book Revision in the Church of England*, ch. 2; C. O.
Buchanan, 'Prayer Book Revision in England 1906-1965', in
Towards a Modern Prayer Book, ed. R. T. Beckwith.

13. ' "This Bread and this Cup": an Evangelical Rejoinder,' by
R. T. Beckwith and C. O. Buchanan, in *Theology*, vol. 70, no. 564
(June 1967), p. 266f.   Drury died early in 1926, but it seems from
*Walter Howard Frere: his Correspondence on Liturgical Revision and
Construction* (ed. R. C. D. Jasper, London, SPCK for Alcuin Club,
1954) that he had ceased to be active in Prayer Book revision
about 1920, the year when he resigned the see of Ripon.
Mitchell's liturgy was printed in *The Churchman*, vol. 43, no. 1
(January 1929), under the title *A Liturgical Essay*. We are
indebted to the Rev. G. W. Grubb for drawing our attention to
it.

14. The *Evangelical Eucharist* was drawn up and circulated in 1963.
An account of it appeared in *Studia Liturgica*, vol. 3, no. 3 (Winter
1964).

2 Doctrinal Issues in Revision

◇◇◇

The Meaning of the Eucharist

AMONG modern liturgiologists, clear, biblical thinking is not as common as one could wish. Their interests are usually historical rather than theological, and they tend to understand 'worship' and 'liturgy' in the narrower sense of those words, as expressions of an attitude to God, with an insufficient appreciation of the Pauline insistence that all worship must be edifying to men, in order that it may be truly corporate (1 Cor. 14. 1-33). Corporateness, as an ideal for worship, is indeed much in vogue, but it is often thought of as a joint participation in the action of the sacraments, and as a spirit of togetherness resulting from this, rather than as a joint intellectual activity, resulting from verbal and symbolical instruction. The unselfish primitive eucharist, which A. H. Couratin (the reputed drafter of Series 2) takes as his aim, gets teaching and petition over in the Antecommunion, but is loath to introduce into the Communion proper any self-regarding idea (even penitence or the benefits of the sacrament) in order that there may be undistracted concentration on praise and thanksgiving.[1] Couratin is very attracted by E. C. Ratcliff's theory about the original form of the consecration prayer in the *Apostolic Tradition* of Hippolytus. According to this theory, the original text, unlike that extant, had no epiclesis (invocation of the Holy Spirit) but it did have a *Sanctus*; and the *Sanctus* was not in the position familiar since the fourth century, quite early in the prayer, but right at the end.[2]   The concluding note was therefore one of praise to God in concert with the whole company of heaven.   Ratcliff links his theory with the New Testament doctrine, taken up by Irenaeus, that our altar and temple are in heaven; and Couratin adds also the narrative of Ex. 24. 1-11 about the sacrifice of the Old Covenant and the feast upon it eaten and drunk by the elders of Israel in the presence of God on the mount; inferring that, in a parallel way, the thankoffering of Christ's body and blood in the eucharist is our 'ticket of admission' to the worship of heaven, where we join in praising God in the words of the *Sanctus*, and in his presence partake of Christ's body and blood.[3]   This speculation explains why Couratin was so concerned that the consecration prayer of Series 2 should say 'we offer unto thee this bread and this cup',[4] and why the prayer still goes on to say 'we eat and drink these holy gifts in the presence of your divine majesty'.

Couratin's romantic picture of the early eucharist seems to be based less on Scripture or history than on subjective religious experience, and a little reflection shows that it is replete with difficulties and contradictions.   In the first place, thanksgiving and the desire to be admitted to the worship of heaven are both self-regarding, no less than edification, petition, penitence and the benefits of the sacrament.   If Couratin is right, the Communion proper ought to consist exclusively of abstract praise. In the second place, the most ancient eucharistic thanksgivings (dating from the late first century onwards) include petition. Not only is there the petition for the Spirit in the extant text of Hippolytus's prayer, but petition occurs in the eucharistic prayers of the *Didache* (chs. 9 and 10), which for good measure requires that confession of sins shall precede them (ch. 14); and petition likewise occurs in the eucharistic prayers which Couratin thinks to be reflected in 1 Clement and in that described by Justin Martyr (*First Apology*, chs. 65, 67).   In the third place, if the eucharistic sacrifice is our 'ticket of admission' to heaven, it is a propitiatory sacrifice, not just a thankoffering.

27

In the fourth place, Couratin's whole conception of the unselfish eucharist is Pelagian, in the traditional sense of the word. It misconceives Christian prayer (which in the New Testament consists primarily of asking); it underestimates our need for divine grace; and it forgets that a sacrament, whatever else it may be, is basically one of the prime means through which divine grace is received.

From these cloudy and inconsistent ideas about the Godward orientation of the eucharist, it is no great step to the Liturgical Commission's principle of deliberate ambiguity on eucharistic doctrine. This principle bids fair to justify the Lutheran charge that, according to Anglicans, people may believe what they like, provided they use the same liturgy. The introduction to Series 2 stated that

> We have also, where matters of eucharistic doctrine are concerned, tried to produce forms of words which are capable of various interpretations. . . . Only by using such language as does not require any one interpretation can we produce a liturgy which all will be able to use, and which each will be able to interpret according to his own convictions (*An Order for Holy Communion*, London, SPCK, 1966, p. viii).

In a similar strain, R. C. D. Jasper, the chairman of the Liturgical Commission, has written that the only doctrines which the Communion service needs to safeguard by unambiguous language are 'the fundamental essentials' (which he does not define); beyond these, 'there must be studied ambiguity', such as will accommodate every school of thought about the eucharist, from 'those who take their stand by the Reformation' to 'those who believe in an objective real presence of Christ in the elements and in a propitiatory sacrifice for the living and the departed' ('Gore on Liturgical Revision', in the *Church Quarterly Review*, vol. 166, no. 358, January 1965, pp. 27f., 33f.). The introduction to Series 2 specified the request that the bread and wine 'may be unto us' the body and blood of Christ as an example of this deliberate ambiguity in the service, and the chairman of the Commission in his article specified the request 'accept our sacrifice of praise', observing:

What is it that we offer—Christ? ourselves, our souls and bodies? the bread and the cup? our sacrifice of praise and thanksgiving? Some would take this last phrase quite literally—we sincerely offer our praises and thanksgivings to God: others would take it to refer to the sacrifice of Christ himself—a praiseworthy and eucharistic sacrifice. The last two are phrases which we should be well advised to use, leaving people to interpret them as they will.

The Commission's words drew from G.B. Timms the comment:

I am by no means certain that the principle, 'let us use ambiguous language which each will be able to interpret according to his own convictions', is a praiseworthy one. It comes perilously near a dishonouring of truth and a prostitution of language, which is meant to express thought rather than to veil it. . . . For my own part I have sufficient confidence in the rationality of man and in the maxim, *magna est veritas et praevalebit*, to believe that, if in charity and openmindedness we lay bare our hearts and thoughts to one another, we shall be led to a common mind which can find satisfying liturgical expression (*Church Times*, 14 January 1966).

The reaction of Evangelicals was similar.[5]

If there *is* to be a dialogue between Catholics and Evangelicals on the doctrine of the eucharist and its expression in liturgy, an attempt to anticipate its results in this book would be to nullify the enterprise. All that can be done at this stage is to make a contribution to the debate. But the following points are certainly some of the chief which Evangelicals would wish to make.

1. If *corporate worship must be edifying*, as St. Paul declares, then needless ambiguity is not a virtue but a vice. Those who aim to teach nothing in particular can easily end up teaching nothing at all.

2. If we are to get back behind the eucharistic controversies of history, as the Liturgical Commission desires, we must go back not just to the supposed original text of Hippolytus, but to *the New Testament itself*. The unsophisticated forms of language used by the earliest Fathers are not intrinsically better than the more carefully safeguarded forms which were thought out in

response to heresy—indeed they may be worse, as in the cases of Trinitarian and Christological doctrine. But the forms of language used in the New Testament, and the ideas behind them, are not only older still, but are normative. They provide a standard by which the eucharistic controversies of history can be judged and (if they can be resolved) settled. At all events, no school of thought could object to the aim of returning, as far as possible, to the language which the New Testament uses, provided this language was used in its completeness, and was not isolated from its context and applied in arbitrary ways.

3. Turning, therefore, to the New Testament, the Holy Communion was instituted at *the time of the passover* and against that background—if not, indeed, at the passover meal itself. The service ought consequently to contain at least an allusion to the passover, such as the 1662 proper preface for Easter or the statement of Series 2-3 that Christ '*freed* us from the *slavery* of sin'.

4. The Holy Communion makes direct reference to *the death of Christ*. 'This is my body *which is given* for you. . . . This is my blood of the covenant *which is shed* for you and for many for the forgiveness of sins' said our Lord, using present participles of the immediate future, as Jeremias points out.[6] These statements provide the background against which our Lord went on to say 'Do this in commemoration of *me*', and St. Paul therefore gives the natural sense of the command when he quite deliberately expounds it in the words 'For as often as you eat this bread and drink the cup you proclaim the Lord's *death*' (1 Cor. 11. 25f.). It is necessary to insist on this because much modern literature on the atonement (the unbiblical tendency of which is potently demonstrated in the writings of Leon Morris)[7] has sought to take the emphasis off Christ's death, and either to transfer it to the resurrection and heavenly session or to spread it over all his mighty acts. Liturgiologists have been strongly affected by this tendency. In his address to the Minneapolis Anglican Congress, the former

chairman of the Liturgical Commission, Bishop D. C. Dunlop, alleged that the restriction of Christ's sacrifice to his death, as we find it in the Book of Common Prayer, is of medieval origin.[8] The same charge recurs in *Re-Shaping the Liturgy*, by H. de Candole and A. H. Couratin (p. 30). The subcommittee on the Book of Common Prayer at the 1958 Lambeth Conference, of which Bishop Dunlop was a leading member, wrote: 'The sacrifice of Christ as the offering of willing obedience included not only his death on the Cross but all that contributed to it, of which it was the culmination. The finished work of Calvary is consummated in the resurrection and ascension' (*The Lambeth Conference 1958*, p. 2:84). If the only effect of this teaching on liturgy were that thanks were given for Christ's other mighty acts as well as his death, one could not reasonably complain, but when the special reference of the sacrament to Christ's death is seriously obscured, as it was in Series 2, then it is time for those who love the gospel to protest. A considerable improvement is evident in Series 3, but there is still some way to go before the service gets back to the splendid and repeated emphasis on the centrality of the cross which was laid by Cranmer, especially in the exhortations, in the words of administration and, above all, in the consecration prayer. In our revision of Series 2-3, we have attempted to restore this emphasis.

5. The Holy Communion represents Christ's death as *an act of atonement:* 'given *for you . . .* shed *for you and for many for the forgiveness of sins*'. Similarly, it represents his death as *a covenant sacrifice:* 'This is my blood *of the covenant*, which is shed for many' or 'This cup is *the New Covenant* in my blood'. It is not just Christ's death, but these aspects of Christ's death that the Holy Communion makes central, and it is these aspects therefore, that should be prominently reflected in the liturgy. Both, of course, are explicit in the institution narrative, and the former has great emphasis in other parts of 1662, though somewhat less in Series 2-3, which has led us to attempt strengthening Series 2-3 at this point. The covenant aspect of Christ's death

could certainly receive additional mention both in 1662 and in Series 2-3, though the gospel feast, of which 1662 speaks in the second exhortation and Series 2-3 in the sentences from 1 Cor. 10. 16f. accompanying the fraction, is really a covenant conception, which the sacramental actions dramatically underline.

6. The Holy Communion looks forward to *the second coming of Christ and the final establishment of God's kingdom.* 'I will not eat it, *until it be fulfilled in the kingdom of God.* . . . I will not drink henceforth of this fruit of the vine, *until that day when I drink it new with you in my Father's kingdom',* said our Lord. 'You proclaim the Lord's death *till he come,'* said St. Paul. The Prayer Book service is often alleged to be deficient in eschatology, either future or realised,[9] but one must not underestimate the importance of the phrase 'until his coming again' in the consecration prayer, or of the teaching in the postcommunion Prayer of Thanksgiving that one of the effects of the sacrament is assurance that we are 'heirs, through hope, of thy everlasting kingdom'. Moreover, the words of administration and the conclusion of the Prayer of Humble Access are genuine expressions of realised eschatology (not a twentieth century discovery altogether), and there are incidental eschatological references elsewhere. The same deficiency in eschatology has been alleged against Series 2,[10] and perhaps with more reason, though Series 3 shows a marginal improvement, and we have attempted to improve it still further, notably in the prayer of consecration.

7. The Holy Communion invites us to '*eat*' of Christ's '*body*' given for us and to '*drink*' of his '*blood*' shed for us. The sixth chapter of St. John's Gospel teaches that to eat Christ's flesh and drink his blood confer the benefits of oneness with Christ, everlasting life and the hope of a joyful resurrection (vv. 53f., 56-58). These truths are prominent both in 1662 and in Series 2 (though the hope of the resurrection is not explicit in Series 3, as an effect of the sacrament).

It is here, however, that one of the most controversial points of eucharistic doctrine arises, and it is out of the question for us to ignore it, because of its liturgical consequences. The point is that, though there is in the eucharist a real partaking of Christ's body and blood, it is possible to conceive of this occurring with or without a real presence of his body and blood in the elements. For 'This is my body' need not be taken literally, but could very well be understood to mean 'This represents my body', like the interpretative words at the Jewish passover, or the similar phrases in Mt. 13. 37-39 and other passages of the Bible. In the same way, the sin of 'not distinguishing the body', and the physical judgments which it is liable to bring (1 Cor. 11. 29-31), can be paralleled from the corresponding judgments incurred by profaning the sacred feasts of the Old Testament, in which no one imagines there to be a bodily presence of the Lord in the elements (Lev. 7. 20f.; 22. 3). That we are *not* to think of a real presence of Christ's body and blood in the eucharistic elements is suggested by Heb. 13. 9-12, where it is apparently asserted that, though Christians eat of Christ's sacrifice, they ought to concern themselves with grace, not with foods. It is likewise suggested by the fact that in the parallel case of baptism, and in the comparable cases of the Old Testament ceremonies which the sacraments replaced, grace accompanies the action, but the Lord is not located in a static fashion in the elements. And it is very strongly suggested by the sixth chapter of St. John, where the same effects (everlasting life and the hope of the resurrection) are attributed both to the participation of Christ's flesh and blood (vv. 53f., 57f.) and to faith in him and his words (vv. 40, 44, 47, 63f., 68f.); where it is explained that Christ is to ascend, that it is the Spirit who gives life and that the flesh is of no profit (vv. 60-63); and where the Jewish background concerns the personified divine Wisdom, who is eaten and drunk not through tangible foods but through the words of the Scriptures (see Ecclesiasticus 24. 21, 23).

It seems from this that the Anglican Reformers were right at least to discourage all beliefs and practices which imply, or strongly suggest, the presence of Christ's body and blood in the elements. Such are the belief that the wicked partake of Christ's body and blood (condemned in Article 29), the practice of adoration (condemned in the declaration on kneeling or Black Rubric)[11] and the practice of reservation (excluded by the rubric about the disposal of the remains, which from 1552 onwards directed that they revert to ordinary use, and from 1662 onwards that they be consumed at the end of the service). Articles 25 and 28 also allude to adoration and reservation, but their language is considered by lawyers too indirect to decide these questions. Consequently, the attitude of the Anglican formularies to these two practices, which are sufficiently controversial to have caused the defeat of the 1928 Prayer Book, and which Catholic revisers of the Prayer Book abroad have been more cautious of introducing than any other change, depends on what happens to the Black Rubric and the rubric about the disposal of the remains. If the future of the 1662 service were clear, or if the rubrics of Series 2-3 conformed to those of 1662, it would be easier to see where we stand. As it is, however, no official steps have yet been taken to modernize the 1662 service, and the recent report *Church and State* (London, CIO, 1970, pp. 24-26, 99) has raised the question whether, after the expiry of the Alternative Services Measure, its use should be permitted in any form. Meanwhile, in Series 2-3, the Black Rubric has been dropped, and the rubric on the consumption of the remains has been altered in a way which, it has been ruled in the courts, legalises reservation.[12] It is, of course, true that the Liturgical Commission had a *prima facie* reason for omitting the Black Rubric, in that the Rubric takes its cue from kneeling, which Series 2-3 does not prescribe. But it would have been easy to adapt the Rubric to cover other postures, and their main reason for omitting it was doubtless their declared policy of ambiguity on eucharistic doctrine. Another objection to the retention of the rubric could be that it speaks of heaven under the unfashionable analogy of a place, but since this is the biblical analogy, there

34

is reason to think that fashion will change, just as Cullmann's influence has led it to change on a closely related issue— whether one may speak of eternity in terms of time. As regards reservation, the curious thing is that it has been legalised by mistake. It was never discussed by Church Assembly, who had no idea that it was involved in Series 2, and the Liturgical Commission's *Commentary on Holy Communion Series 3* (p. 27) states that, though they have retained the rubric on the disposal of the remains in what is essentially its Series 2 form, they are not aiming at an alteration of the law. The fact remains that they have altered it. Both these changes in Series 2-3 have therefore had to be challenged at the national level (*Church Assembly Report*, vol. 47, no. 3, Summer 1967, p. 542f.; *General Synod Report*, vol. 1, no. 1, Autumn 1970, p. 72), and in the revision here published the substance of the 1662 rubrics is restored (1662 Revised, para. 29; Series 2-3 Revised, para. 33; Appendix).

8. From one controversy, it is necessary to pass on to another. The Holy Communion, as we find it in the New Testament, *contains no statement or act indicating that any sacrifice is being offered in the service, except the giving of thanks.* Our Lord gave thanks (said grace) over the bread and wine, and thanksgiving or praise is elsewhere in the New Testament stated to be one of the spiritual sacrifices which are offered by the priesthood of all believers (Heb. 13. 15). The gospels do not actually say that our Lord 'offered the sacrifice of praise', and *we* ought not to say it if it is going to be interpreted in the double sense indicated by the Liturgical Commission and Dr. Jasper in the passages quoted at the beginning of the chapter. If we do use this phrase, therefore, we ought not to use it in the consecration prayer (the place where, in unreformed theology, the sacrifice of the mass is conceived to occur) but only in Cranmer's post-communion position, where it cannot be misunderstood.[13] Otherwise it is better simply to say that we give thanks, as the gospels say of our Lord.

Of course, Catholics are accustomed to find sacrifice in the

New Testament account of the eucharist at many other points than this. Sometimes they have found it in our Lord's taking of the bread, which Dix identified with the offertory (see the opening section of chapter three, on 'The Evolution of the Liturgy'), and which thus gave rise to elaborate offertory processions, until the present Primate accused them of reflecting 'a shallow and romantic sort of Pelagianism' (*Durham Essays and Addresses*, London, SPCK, 1956, p. 18)). Since then, they seem to have lost their popularity. In reality, the offertory corresponds to the action of the attendant rather than to that of the Lord, and is no more sacrificial than is waiting at table.

It is astonishing, therefore, that the drafters of Series 3 are attempting to revive the offertory procession. The Series 3 rubrics read as follows:

24. The bread and wine are brought to the holy table.
25. The president takes the bread and wine.

Any doubt that this hints at an offertory procession is dispelled by the report of the joint working party appointed by the Liturgical Commission and the Council for the Care of Churches to advise on the ceremonial of Series 3, where we find the following:

It is well to remember that we have now reached the place in the service where the Bible ceases to be the focal point, and is replaced by the vessels and the elements. It is therefore fitting that their introduction into the rite should be accompanied by some form of offertory procession. . . . These things may be brought to the president *by* the congregation *from* the congregation. . . . It is important that, if the bread and wine are brought to the table as symbolic of the offering of our lives and the fruits of our labours, the collection should also be received at the same time (*The Presentation of the Eucharist*, London, SPCK, 1971, p. 14f.).

It is depressing to see these exploded errors being disinterred.

Catholics also draw attention to the sacrificial language which our Lord, at the Last Supper, used of his body and blood, but this refers to a sacrifice soon to be offered, not offered then and there (see section 4 above). The Lord's Supper is a feast upon that sacrifice, certainly, and can consequently be compared by

St. Paul with feasts upon other sacrifices, Jewish and heathen
(1 Cor. 10. 14-22); but it is not the offering (the slaying or
priestly presentation) of that sacrifice, which in the former
sense took place on the cross, and in the latter sense when
Christ entered the heavenly sanctuary at his ascension.[14] Yet
again, Catholics appeal to the phrase 'Do this in commemoration of me', arguing that 'commemoration' (*anamnesis*) means
'memorial offering', or alternatively 'making present again'
(i.e. of Christ in his sacrificed condition), or even that 'do'
(*poiein*) means 'offer'. This is not the place to detail all the
arguments against these contentions:[15] suffice it to say that the
contentions are extremely doubtful, and that dubious interpretations ought not to be imposed upon the Church in corporate
liturgy. The words ought to be translated according to their
normal meaning, leaving individuals to read in personal
interpretations in their private thoughts. When doing so, they
should always bear in mind that 'Christ dieth no more' (Rom.
6. 9) and that 'there is no more offering for sin' (Heb. 10. 18)—
facts of which the liturgy does well to remind them.

The subcommittee on the Book of Common Prayer at the
1958 Lambeth Conference expressed the opinion that

> as the result of new knowledge gained from biblical and liturgical
> studies the time has come to claim that controversies about the
> Eucharistic Sacrifice can be laid aside, the tensions surrounding
> this doctrine transcended, and the way prepared for the making
> of a liturgy in God's good time which will in its essential structure
> win its way throughout the whole Anglican Communion (*The
> Lambeth Conference 1958*, p. 2:83).

Even when these words were written, there were reasons for
thinking the claim premature, for the subcommittee had before
it two reports from Anglican Churches involved in revision,
the Church of India, Pakistan, Burma and Ceylon and the
Anglican Church of Canada, which showed that disagreements
about the eucharistic sacrifice and its expression in liturgy
were still very much alive.[16] The Canadian report stated that
there had been controversy both over the eucharistic sacrifice
and over prayer for the dead, as expressed in the 1955 draft of

their revision, that in consequence it had been necessary to alter the language relating to the former, and that 'as far as Eucharistic doctrine is concerned, the revisers have been forced to recognise that it is still impossible to find full agreement in our Church'. If this was the situation before the Lambeth subcommittee wrote, time has not mended matters. The subcommittee's own idea of the sort of doctrine of eucharistic sacrifice which Anglicans could now agree to express in liturgy has been criticised by the distinguished Anglo-Catholic theologian, E. L. Mascall, as going beyond Rome, and it has also been criticised by Roman Catholics and by Evangelicals.[17] If its aim had been to evoke disagreement from all sides, it could hardly have done better! Also since 1958, the language in which the Indian revision expressed the eucharistic sacrifice and the commemoration of the departed has had to be toned down considerably, before the service could be finally adopted, and the language used on the same two matters by the Series 2 service in this country has likewise had to be seriously modified, before the service could be adopted even experimentally. It is on the commemoration of the departed that disagreement has centred in Africa, where the province of East Africa has removed the prayer for the dead from the *Liturgy for Africa* before authorising it for use. In Australia, a self-denying ordinance by Catholics in the interests of unity has kept out of the experimental services all innovations which are doctrinally controversial (*Prayer Book Revision in Australia*, p. vi).

While dealing with the eucharistic sacrifice, it may be as well to deal also with prayer for the dead, since they frequently come together in controversy, and have a number of close links. In the first place, they are linked by the fact that prayer for the dead is a normal feature of intercession in the early liturgies, just as an offering of the bread and cup is a normal feature of early consecration prayers. In the second place, neither feature can be shown to be present in the worship of the New Testament. In the third place, both features were struck out of the liturgy by the Anglican Reformers, because of their lack of scriptural backing and the errors with which they had become associated (all that is denoted by the mass, purgatory and—in combination—masses for the dead).[18]   In the fourth place, both have been brought back in many of the Anglican Churches abroad, without any adequate attempt being made to answer the theological objections to them or to guard against the associated errors (to which modern atonement theology and modern universalism are now adding).[19]   What should be our attitude to these two matters?   Surely, if we desire to be truly primitive, if we desire to get back behind the controversies of history and to return to the teaching on the eucharist and on prayer which we find clearly expressed in the New Testament, we ought to be able to agree that in corporate worship we will confine the language of oblation and the language of petition to those matters and to those classes of persons to which the New Testament clearly applies them.   In our private thoughts and our private devotions we are answerable only to God, and must do as we judge best.   But in the outward forms which we use for corporate worship we are answerable also to our neighbour, and unity and concord are imperilled unless we exercise restraint.   This does not mean accepting the Puritan principle that what is not contained in Scripture is prohibited: it only means acting on the unmistakably Anglican principle that what is not contained in Scripture is unessential. Again, it does not mean that in the liturgy we cannot use the language of oblation in ways in which the New Testament uses it, or that we cannot add to the consecration prayer an *anamnesis* which is genuinely a commemoration, or that we cannot remember the faithful departed by giving thanks for their revealed blessedness: we can.   What we cannot do, however, is to say, 'we offer unto thee this bread and this cup', as Series 2 originally said; or to say 'we commend all men (i.e. departed and living, faithful and unfaithful) to your unfailing love, that in them your will may be fulfilled', as Series 3 says; or to substitute something which is simply an ambiguous paraphrase, and is meant to cover the same meaning.

9. The Holy Communion, as we find it in the New Testament, has *a connection with the unity of the Church and with the activity of the Holy Spirit.* The former connection is clearly stated in 1 Cor. 10. 17, and the latter connection is clearly hinted at in Jn. 6. 63 and 1 Cor. 10. 4, though neither receives a great deal of attention. It is proper, however, that both these pregnant thoughts should find a place in the liturgy. In 1662, they both occur in the post-communion Prayer of Thanksgiving, and the latter also in the first and third exhortations. In Series 3, they both occur at the end of the consecration prayer, and the former also in the quotation of 1 Cor. 10. 16f. accompanying the fraction.

If the foregoing sections 3 to 9 give a fair account of what the New Testament clearly says about the meaning of the eucharist, and accurately distinguish this from what the New Testament does not clearly say (or even denies), is it not proper to conclude that whatever comes in the former category should be plainly expressed in the liturgy, and that anything which comes in the latter category can very well be omitted, however attractive one may find it, or however old it may be? These are the basic principles on which the service that follows has been drawn up, and its compilers would like to enter into serious dialogue with Catholic Anglicans and others about it. The issues we desire to discuss are whether the account that has been given of the New Testament teaching is a true one, and whether this teaching is adequately expressed in the draft service. If agreement can be reached on these points, the prospects will at once become brighter for a revision of the Anglican liturgy which will unite and not divide.

The Consecration of the Eucharist

THE basis of the idea of the consecration of the bread and wine of the eucharist is the belief that holy communion is a sacrament of the gospel, in which God takes earthly things and uses

40

them as means of saving grace. But different ideas about the way in which God does this give rise to different conceptions of consecration. To the Roman Catholic, consecration implies transubstantiation, and it was apparently because his own views were akin to transubstantiation that the late E. C. Ratcliff could not see that Cranmer believed in the consecration of the elements, despite Cranmer's explicit statement, dating from the very period of the composition of his second Prayer Book, that he did:

> Consecration is the separation of anything from a profane and worldly use unto a spiritual and godly use. And therefore when usual and common water is taken from other uses, and put to the use of baptism in the name of the Father, and of the Son, and of the Holy Ghost, then it may rightly be called consecrated water, that is to say, water put to an holy use. Even so, when common bread and wine be taken and severed from other bread and wine to the use of the holy communion, that portion of bread and wine, although it be of the same substance that the other is from the which it is severed, yet it is now called consecrated, or holy bread and holy wine. Not that the bread and wine have or can have any holiness in them, but that they be used to an holy work, and represent holy and godly things. And therefore S. Dionyse called the bread holy bread, and the cup an holy cup, as soon as they be set upon the altar to the use of the holy communion. But specially they may be called holy and con-secrated, when they be separated to that holy use by Christ's own words, which he spake for that purpose, saying of the bread, 'This is my body', and of the wine, 'This is my blood'. So that commonly the authors, before those words be spoken, do take the bread and wine but as other common bread and wine; but after those words be pronounced over them, then they take them for consecrated and holy bread and wine.[20]

Cranmer did not believe in transubstantiation, but he did believe that the sacrament is a means of grace. Summing up some years of debate on Cranmer's eucharistic theology, Peter Brooks has concluded that the main question in debate, whether Cranmer was a Zwinglian, ought never to have been asked. To present the Zwinglian and Calvinistic views as self-contained and mutually exclusive is to misconceive both and to betray a somewhat superficial understanding of history and theology. Calvin's view is a development of Zwingli's, though an original development, and Cranmer's view is roughly Calvin's, but still reflects independence of mind.[21] Consecration, for Cranmer, means that the elements are set apart in a divinely appointed way to be means of grace to worthy partakers. On this view, therefore, no less than on the Roman Catholic view, the idea is present that the bread and wine when eaten and drunk are not common bread and wine. They are not *in every respect* the same as they were before, but have been made a sacrament. And this is consecration.

The fact that the consecrated elements are means of grace does not mean that consecration is wholly the act of God and in no sense an act of man. The institution is God's and the grace is God's, but the middle term is the performance by man of the instituted rite, which by God's gracious will and promise is the means of his grace to worthy partakers. Again, the question whether consecration is God's act or man's cannot be decided by an appeal to the fact that God alone is holy, and therefore only he is competent to consecrate anything. For the Bible contains many examples of persons whom God has *made* holy, and who consecrate other persons or things by God's *command and authorisation*. This is not to say that such human consecration is not indirectly the act of God, so it is quite meaningful that in the consecration prayer of the 1549 Prayer Book, as in the consecration prayers of some of the early liturgies (St. James, St. Mark, St. Basil), there is a petition that *God* will consecrate the elements, similar to the petition in baptismal liturgies that he will consecrate the water. On the other hand, the rubric after the distribution of the wine in 1662 distinctly speaks of consecration as an act of man, and this is the way that Cranmer deliberately interprets the word in the passage cited above, and the way that it is commonly used by dogmaticians and liturgiologists today. Provided they are referring to man's performance of a consecratory act authorised by God, this usage also is meaningful and legitimate, and it is this usage which will be followed in the remainder of our discussion.

Since, however, man cannot consecrate anything save by authorisation from God, sacramental consecration cannot be located outside the compass of the acts which God has instituted. In baptism, the whole consecration lies in the conferring and receiving of the sacrament—the washing, with its words of explanation—for nothing else is instituted. In holy communion, however, the institution is a little more complex. When our Lord said 'Do this in commemoration of me. . . . Do this, as often as you drink it, in commemoration of me' (Lk. 22. 19; 1 Cor. 11. 24f.), he has sometimes been taken to mean simply 'eat and drink'. The main basis of this idea is St. Paul's explanation in 1 Cor. 11. 26 'For as often as you eat this bread and drink the cup you proclaim the Lord's death'. Notice, however, that St. Paul does not say 'By eating this bread and drinking the cup you proclaim the Lord's death'; and that he does not mean this may be inferred from three facts: (i) that a mere eating of bread and drinking of wine by Christians would hardly 'remind' anyone of Christ, and would certainly not 'proclaim his death'; (ii) that before the command 'Do this', in St. Paul's account, the eating and drinking have not even been mentioned; (iii) that the words 'Do this, as often as you drink it' appear to distinguish the doing from the drinking, as something which accompanies it but is in fact different. It seems, therefore, that those commentators are right who take 'Do this' to mean, not 'Do what you are doing' (eating and drinking), but 'Do what I have done' (taken bread, given thanks, broken it, distributed it, spoken the explanatory words; taken the cup, given thanks, distributed it, spoken the explanatory words). Recently, Cranmer has often been charged with understanding 'Do this' to mean 'eat and drink', and the alleged deficiencies of his services have been explained accordingly. The way that, in the 1552 service, the closing words of the institution narrative 'Do this, as oft as ye shall drink it, in remembrance of me' are immediately followed by the words of administration 'Take and eat this in remembrance that Christ died for thee' lends some slight plausibility to the theory, though it should be observed that the former sentence refers to the cup and the latter to the bread, and that the absence of an 'Amen' in between (a frequent omission of the 1552 Book) is certainly fortuitous. In any case, it is impossible to believe that Cranmer is here giving an exhaustive account of what he understands by 'Do this', for the following reasons:

1. We have already seen, from his own statement about consecration, that Cranmer regarded the repetition of the explanatory words as part of the instituted rite.

2. He did not allow the communicants to help themselves to the bread and wine, which could well mean that he regarded the ministerial taking and distributing as parts of the instituted rite. Indeed, he states elsewhere that it is by Christ's institution that the minister has the office of delivering the elements to the people (*On the Lord's Supper*, Parker Society, pp. 350, 352). The fact that the token acts of taking in the institution narrative disappeared in 1552 may have been due to a fear of encouraging the continuance of elevation, though it is usually attributed to the objections of Bucer. The functional taking, for the purpose of distribution, was of course unaffected.

3. In the 1549 Book Cranmer retained the fraction, and the 1549 Book, as we now know, expresses his mature eucharistic theology. It was mentioned only incidentally, in a rubric which was omitted in 1552 because Gardiner had appealed to it, but there is no sufficient reason to think that Cranmer intended the fraction to cease, which it certainly did not, if one may judge from the strong views of Hooper, Hutchinson, Grindal and Jewel in favour of the practice.[22] One should also note that, in Cranmer's writings on the eucharist, 1 Cor. 10. 16, 'the bread which *we break*', is one of his favourite texts, and he speaks of how the believer 'cometh to the Lord's Supper, and (*according to Christ's commandment*) receiveth the bread *broken*, in remembrance that Christ's body was broken for him upon the cross' (*On the Lord's Supper*, Parker Society, p. 36).

The failure to mention the fraction in the 1552 Book must therefore be attributed either to the Book's general sparseness in rubrics, or (as before) to a fear of encouraging the continuance of elevation, but not to a desire that the fraction should cease.[23]

4. As regards the remaining action, the giving of thanks, which is so widely regarded as Cranmer's blind spot,[24] the mere fact that in 1552 he separated the *Sanctus* from the prayer containing the institution narrative is quite immaterial. The importance that he attached to the parts of the service which express thanksgiving is manifest to anyone who reads the 1552 service attentively, for in the third exhortation (which he directed to be read on all occasions, and which is the introduction to the Communion proper) he says that '*above all things*, ye must give most humble and hearty thanks to God'; while, in the Prayer of Oblation, he refers back to the whole service as 'our sacrifice of praise and thanksgiving'. There are also plenty of statements about the place of thanksgiving in the Lord's Supper to be found in his controversial writings (*On the Lord's Supper*, Parker Society, pp. 352, 361f., 366 etc.).

If these, then, together with the eating and drinking, are the constituents of the rite which our Lord established, is there any reason why one constituent and not another should be regarded as consecratory? Surely there is not. And though, in ordinary usage, consecration is referred to one or more of the acts preceding or accompanying reception, the eating and drinking are themselves vital parts of the institution, and are therefore likewise consecratory, in the sense that they too put the elements to a holy use and make them means of grace to those who partake worthily.

Of the traditional views about what consecrates, the least defensible is the Eastern view, to which the Nonjurors also approximated, that consecration is effected by petition, and more particularly by the petition (known as the epiclesis) that the Holy Spirit may descend upon the elements or the worshippers. Petition may appropriately accompany the instituted acts

45

(seeing that the sacrament is a means of God's grace, for which we may properly ask), and it has been included in consecration prayers, as we saw at the beginning of this chapter, since the end of the first century. The earliest actual epiclesis that we know of, occurring in a consecration prayer, is that in the *Apostolic Tradition* of Hippolytus (early third century), though the authenticity of Hippolytus's epiclesis is disputed.[25] From the fourth century, the epiclesis became normal in Eastern liturgies, but it never had a place in the Roman liturgy till our own day, when three new alternative consecration prayers have been added to the mass, each containing not just one epiclesis but two! However, despite the antiquity and prevalence of the epiclesis, the still greater antiquity of petition in some form, and the undeniable appropriateness of the latter, it is not one of the instituted acts, and therefore cannot rightly be held to consecrate.

The view that is fashionable today is that what consecrates is the giving of thanks.[26] This view has in its favour that thanksgiving is at least one of the instituted acts. Its supporters point out that the early consecration prayers, from Hippolytus onwards, regularly open with thanksgiving, and that, still earlier, the *Didache* (chs. 9f., 14) and Justin Martyr (*First Apology*, chs. 65-67) seem to lay special stress on the thanksgiving. They go on to claim that consecration by thanksgiving can be traced right back to the New Testament, where grace at meat is stated in 1 Tim. 4. 3-5, following Jewish ideas, to sanctify it. But this claim seems to be based on a confusion of terms. 'Sanctify' in relation to grace at meat is biblical language, and means 'acknowledge something as already holy' (because created by God). 'Consecrate' in relation to holy communion is ecclesiastical language, and means 'make something holy in a way it was not before' (as a means of grace). Jn. 6. 23 can also be invoked, though a miracle of quite a different kind is in view there, and however efficacious the thanksgiving of Jesus may have been on that occasion, we cannot necessarily expect our own thanksgiving at holy communion to have equal efficacy with the thanksgiving of the Son of God. The most that can be claimed with any certainty is that thanksgiving is one of the instituted acts, and that it was early believed to play an important part in the consecration of the elements.

The last of the traditional views (for no one seems anxious to make the taking, breaking and distributing the consecratory acts) is that the consecratory act is the recital of our Lord's interpretative words. This is the old Roman view, going back possibly to Tertullian (*Against Marcion* 4. 40) in the early third century. It is also the traditional Anglican view, as Ratcliff shows in the articles cited in note 20; the view of many of the Reformers, including Cranmer, as is shown by the last two sentences of the quotation from Cranmer at the beginning of this section of the chapter; the view suggested by the directions on supplementary consecration in the 1637 Scottish and 1662 English Prayer Books; and the view held by a few writers even today, notably by A. H. Couratin.[27] The reason why this view appealed to Cranmer and the other Reformers is doubtless that it stresses the power of God's word: by the recital of our Lord's words, the elements are (not transubstantiated, but) set apart to be means of grace to worthy communicants. The recital of our Lord's words, like the giving of thanks, is one of the instituted acts, and therefore does have a share in the consecration. The objection that in form they are words of administration not of consecration can be countered by the parallel of Jn. 4. 50, 53, where words in the indicative are similarly words of power. And though what was said of Jn. 6. 23 above applies also to Jn. 4. 50, 53, that we cannot necessarily expect our own use of such words at holy communion to have equal efficacy with the use made of them by the Son of God, yet there is one good reason for thinking that the singling out of the recital of our Lord's words as the *main* consecratory act accompanying reception is right. This is that all the other instituted actions (the manual acts and giving of thanks) were normal in a Jewish meal: they are found, for example, in the feeding of the

47

five thousand, in St. Paul's meal just before being shipwrecked, and in the account of the Passover meal in the Mishnah. The thing that differentiates this meal from any other meal on the Jewish pattern, and so turns a common meal into a sacrament, is the recital of our Lord's interpretative words.

If, then, it be asked whether Cranmer's belief in consecration by the recital of our Lord's words was wrong, the answer is that it was not. Nor was it wrong of the 1662 revisers to prefix the title 'Prayer of Consecration' to that prayer in Cranmer's service which contains the recital of our Lord's words, as part of the institution narrative. Since, however, this is the main part of the truth about consecration rather than the whole of the truth about it, it would seem wiser to put the heading 'The Consecration of the Sacrament' before the whole section beginning with the *Sanctus*, so that the thanksgiving may be included as well, and this is what has been done in the First Text of the Communion (1662 Revised) which is here published. Of course, in cases where the thanksgiving has been joined up again with the prayer containing the institution narrative, such as Series 2-3 and the revision of it here published, the resultant prayer can very well be thought of as the prayer of consecration. But it always needs to be remembered that even this is not the whole of consecration, since the manual acts likewise have a part in it, and the reception itself is in reality a vital consecrating action.

Notes

1. 'The Eucharist under Revision,' in *Tell Wales*, pp. 47, 50; 'Thanksgiving and Thankoffering', in *Studia Liturgica*, vol. 3, no. 1 (Summer 1964), p. 56f. For a liturgiologist who does appreciate the importance of edification in worship, see G. W. O. Addleshaw, *The High Church Tradition: a Study in the Liturgical Thought of the Seventeenth Century* (London, Faber, 1941), ch. 3 'Edification'.
2. 'The Sanctus and the Pattern of the Early Anaphora,' in the *Journal of Ecclesiastical History*, vol. 1, nos. 1 and 2 (April and

October 1950). For the basis of this reconstruction, as regards the exclusion of the epiclesis, see note 25. As regards the addition of the *Sanctus*, its main basis is that without it the prayer ends (so Ratcliff judges) in an anticlimax, and that a consecration prayer ending with the *Sanctus* is mentioned by a Syrian Father of the fifth to sixth centuries (see Ratcliff's further article 'A Note on the Anaphoras described in the Liturgical Homilies of Narsai', in *Biblical and Patristic Studies in memory of R. P. Casey*, ed. J. N. Birdsall and R. W. Thomson, Freiburg, Herder, 1963). For the case against Ratcliff's reconstruction and in favour of the extant text, see the note by Henry Chadwick in *The Apostolic Tradition of S. Hippolytus of Rome*, ed. Gregory Dix (2nd ed., London, SPCK, 1968), pp. k-m. It is perhaps worth adding that the consecration prayer ending with the *Sanctus*, which Narsai describes, includes an epiclesis, so is not in all respects helpful to Ratcliff's case.

3. 'The Sacrifice of Praise,' in *Theology*, vol. 58, no. 422 (August 1955); *Ways of Worship*, ed. P. Edwall, E. Hayman and W. D. Maxwell (London, SCM, 1951), pp. 192-94; 'The Eucharist under Revision', in *Tell Wales*, pp. 50-53; 'Liturgy', in *The Pelican Guide to Modern Theology*, ed. R. P. C. Hanson, vol. 2, pp. 138f., 151-54.

4. ' "We offer unto Thee this Bread and this Cup": the Tradition Received,' in *Theology*, vol. 69, no. 556 (October 1966). Cp. also 'Liturgy', p. 239.

5. See R. T. Beckwith and C. O. Buchanan, ' "This Bread and this Cup": an Evangelical Rejoinder', in *Theology*, vol. 70, no. 564 (June 1967), p. 271; C. O. Buchanan, 'The Place of Ambiguity in Schemes for Reunion', in *The Churchman*, vol. 81, no. 3 (Autumn 1967), p. 172.

6. Joachim Jeremias, *The Eucharistic Words of Jesus* (2nd English ed., London, SCM, 1966), p. 178f.

7. *The Apostolic Preaching of the Cross* (3rd ed., London, Tyndale Press, 1965); *The Cross in the New Testament* (Exeter, Paternoster Press, not dated).

8. 'The Liturgical Life of the Anglican Communion in the Twentieth Century,' in *Report of the Anglican Congress 1954*, p. 90. Cp. Gregory Dix, *The Shape of the Liturgy*, pp. 242, 625. It is quite true that the central importance of Christ's death is not recognised by every early Father or in every ancient liturgy; in this, however, they were not more biblical than the medievals but less.

9. See, for example, Gregory Dix, *The Shape of the Liturgy*, pp. 621f., 626; M. H. Shepherd Jr., 'Our Anglican Understanding of Corporate Worship', in *Report of the Anglican Congress 1954*, p. 84.

10. See, for example, U. E. Simon, 'Unliturgical Remarks on Eucharistic Liturgy', in *Theology*, vol. 74, no. 611 (May 1971), p. 203f.

11. On the meaning of the Black Rubric, see R. T. Beckwith, *Priesthood and Sacraments*, p. 62f. On its history, see. J. T. Tomlinson, *The Prayer Book, Articles and Homilies* (London, Elliot Stock, 1897), ch. 11. See also E. C. Ratcliff, 'The Savoy Conference and the Revision of the Book of Common Prayer', in *From Uniformity to Unity 1662-1962*, ed. G. F. Nuttall and O. Chadwick (London, SPCK, 1962), pp. 139-141.

12. The first case in which reservation was declared lawful on the basis of the Series 2 rubric was In re S. Peter and S. Paul Leckhampton, on 21 and 22 October 1967 (*Weekly Law Reports*, 1968, pt. 2, pp. 1551-55), but there have been others since. A full account of the legal position appears in *The Churchman*, vol. 85, no. 3 (Autumn 1971), in an article entitled 'Do the Alternative Services Legalise Reservation?' On the general question of reservation, see J. A. Motyer and J. I. Packer, *Reservation* (London, Church Book Room Press, 1960).

13. In the Book of Common Prayer, the meaning of the phrase is further brought out by its reappearance in non-eucharistic contexts: see the second Thanksgiving for Deliverance from the Plague, in the Occasional Prayers and Thanksgivings, and the first Collect of Thanksgiving after a Storm, in the Prayers to be Used at Sea. It is not without significance for one's understanding of seventeenth century theology that these two prayers were added in 1604 and 1662 respectively. Of course, in the Septuagint and in unreformed liturgy the phrase is used differently. The Prayer Book use of it is based on Heb. 13. 15.

14. See R. T. Beckwith, *Priesthood and Sacraments*, pp. 87-90, and the literature there cited.

15. For the case against these interpretations, as also against the attempt to correlate the eucharist with Christ's heavenly priesthood, or to merge the spiritual sacrifices and priesthood of Christians with the sacrifice and priesthood of Christ, on which they depend for their acceptance, see *Eucharistic Sacrifice*, ed. J. I. Packer (London, Church Book Room Press, 1962); R. T. Beckwith, *Priesthood and Sacraments*.

16. See *Principles of Prayer Book Revision: the Report of a Select Committee of the CIPBC* (London, SPCK, 1958), pp. 47-50; *A Statement on Prayer Book Revision in Canada* (no publisher's name, place or date), pp. 4-6. The latter document was drawn up by Bishop (later Archbishop) H. H. Clark, at the request of the House of Bishops.

17. See E. L. Mascall, 'Note on the Eucharistic Sacrifice', in A. H. Couratin, *Lambeth and Liturgy* (London, Church Union, 1959), p. 15; Francis Clark, *Eucharistic Sacrifice and the Reformation* (2nd ed., Oxford, Blackwell, 1967), pp. 519-522; J. I. Packer, *Eucharistic Sacrifice*, pp. 1-21.

18. This was not a complete innovation. Prior to the ninth century, there had for several hundred years been no commemoration of the dead whatever at public celebrations of the Roman mass. See Edmund Bishop, *Liturgica Historica* (Oxford, Clarendon Press, 1918), pp. 109-115.

The idea that implicit prayers for the dead have always been retained in the Prayer Book is contrary to the known beliefs of the Edwardian and Elizabethan Reformers and to the teaching of the Book of Homilies ('Homily concerning Prayer', pt. 3), and did not arise until the seventeenth century. The most plausible evidence alleged is the prayer before the Collect in the Burial service, where the phrase 'we with this our brother and all other departed in the true faith of thy holy name' is interpreted as meaning 'we and this our brother', not 'we, like this our brother'. But in actual fact the wording of this prayer, which had been a straightforward petition for the dead in 1549, was completely altered in 1552, presumably to conform it to the Reformers' mature convictions on the subject. The contention that the addition of similar language to the Prayer for the Church Militant in 1662 made a change in the attitude of the Church of England is much less plausible. Even the Laudian reviser Cosin, who approved of prayer for the dead, did not by this stage in his life suppose that the language of the Prayer Book implied it (*Works*, Library of Anglo-Catholic Theology, vol. 5, p. 477). The other Laudian reviser Wren was opposed to prayer for the dead, but they both wanted thanksgiving for the dead added to the prayer, and this sufficiently explains the proposal to omit the words 'militant here in earth' (see G. J. Cuming, *The Durham Book*, London, OUP, 1961, paras 221, 224). In any case, the committee of revisers was not dominated by Cosin and Wren (see p.19 above), and the words 'militant here in earth' were ultimately restored, thus fixing the interpretation of the disputed form of language.

19. For the various forms in which they have been restored, and an analysis of the meaning of these forms, see R. T. Beckwith, *Prayer Book Revision and Anglican Unity* (London, Church Book Room Press, 1967), pp. 12-21.

20. *On the Lord's Supper* (Parker Society), p. 177; also in *The Work of Thomas Cranmer* (Appleford, Sutton Courtenay Press, 1964), p. 181f. See further pp. 11, 131 and the whole of pp. 177-183 in the Parker Society edition. Ratcliff's case is set out in his articles 'The English Usage of Eucharistic Consecration 1548-1662', in *Theology*, vol. 60, nos. 444, 445 (June and July 1957), pp. 233-36. His strongest arguments are that in the 1552 Prayer Book the minister has to his own use whatever bread and wine remain at the end of the service, and that in neither of the Edwardian Prayer Books is there any provision for supplementary consecration if the bread and wine run out. It must be borne in mind, however, that the rubrics of Cranmer's Prayer Books, as compared with those of 1662, are sparse, so further consecration (which was a known practice) may not be excluded by not being mentioned, any more than it is excluded by not being mentioned in Series 1, Series 2 or the service printed below; and that a view of consecration which excludes reservation, and thus sets apart for a holy use such bread and wine as is needed here and now, does not necessarily imply that any which may have to be added is unconsecrated, still less that any which may be left over remains consecrated.

21. *Thomas Cranmer's Doctrine of the Eucharist: an Essay in Historical Development* (London, Macmillan, 1965). An interesting footnote to the debate is D. S. Ross, 'Hooper's Alleged Authorship of A Brief and Clear Confession of the Christian Faith', in *Church History*, vol. 39, no. 1 (March 1970).

22. See Hooper, *Early Writings*, pp. 61, 180, 534; *Later Writings*, p. 145; Hutchinson, *Works*, p. 267; Grindal, *Remains*, p. 42; Jewel, *Works*, vol. 1, p. 127 (all Parker Society editions). It should be noted that the passage from Hooper's *Later Writings* belongs to 1551 or 1552, the passage from Hutchinson to 1552, and the passage from Grindal probably to an earlier period than that from Jewel, to whom Ratcliff, in the second of his articles on 'The English Usage of Eucharistic Consecration 1548-1662' (p. 276), gives the credit for first perceiving Cranmer's 'mistake' on the matter.

23. See J. T. Tomlinson, *The Prayer Book, Articles and Homilies*, p. 218f.
24. See, for example, *Prayer Book Revision in the Church of England*, p. 31; M. J. Moreton, 'The Sacrifice of Praise', in *Church Quarterly Review*, vol. 165, no. 357 (October 1964), p. 491.
25. On the general question of the original form of Hippolytus's consecration prayer, see note 2 above. The main grounds on which his epiclesis has been challenged are that it is absent from one of the dependant documents, the *Testament of our Lord*, that it comes in a work a century older than any other epiclesis extant, and that *Apostolic Tradition* 23. 1 implies consecration by thanksgiving, which is an earlier view, traceable in Justin Martyr. Chadwick has answered the first two arguments, and the third can be answered by pointing out that there is no contradiction, since the epiclesis is included in a prayer of thanksgiving. A parallel is presented by *Apostolic Tradition* 5 and 6, where the bishop is bidden to 'give thanks as at the oblation of bread and wine', but the forms prescribed for him to use are basically petitionary. It should be remembered that a great variety of views on consecration were current in the early Church: see G. A. Michell, *Eucharistic Consecration in the Primitive Church* (London, SPCK, 1948).
26. See, for example, *Prayer Book Revision in the Church of England*, pp. 21f., 31, 33; *The Lambeth Conference 1958*, p. 2.85; H. de Candole and A. H. Couratin, *Re-Shaping the Liturgy*, p. 28.
27. *Lambeth and Liturgy*, p. 11f.; 'The Eucharist under Revision', in *Tell Wales*, p. 49; 'Revising the Eucharist', in *The Liturgical Congress at Carmarthen* (Penarth, Church in Wales Publications, 1965), p. 27. Presumably Couratin is not responsible for the statement on p. 28 of *Re-shaping the Liturgy* about consecration by thanksgiving.

3 Liturgical Issues in Revision

<hr>

The Evolution of the Liturgy

OUR Lord's instituting acts, as we have seen, were nine in number. He took the bread, gave thanks, broke it, distributed it, spoke the interpretative words; then, at the end of the meal, some time afterwards, he took the cup of wine, gave thanks, distributed it, and spoke the interpretative words. So long as the eucharist remained joined to an agape meal, this pattern could continue unimpeded. In the *Didache*, the eucharist is still joined to an agape, and thanks are still given separately over the bread and the cup, though in reverse order, and there is an additional thanksgiving after all the eating and drinking have finished (chs. 9, 10). As soon as the eucharist became separated from the agape, however, the two parts of the sacramental action automatically came together, and since the themes of the two thanksgivings were similar (bodily food, and the salvation which they betokened, corresponding to the themes of the thanksgivings which seem to have been said at the passover meal, and of those in the *Didache*),[1] it was natural to combine them into one thanksgiving for creation and redemption. This had the further practical advantage that, for the reception of the elements, the congregation would only need to approach the Lord's table, or to be approached by the ministers, once not twice. Included in the thanksgiving for redemption, one might expect to find thanksgiving for the institution of the sacrament, and if this embraced the institution narrative itself, it would serve the additional purposes of performing the necessary recital of our Lord's interpretative words,[2] and of furnishing the divine warrant for holding the service. All these features save perhaps thanksgiving for creation may be found in the earliest consecration prayer extant, that in the *Apostolic Tradition* of Hippolytus. The thanksgiving for creation was added in some of the fourth century liturgies, and its sources were much older, since it is mentioned by Justin Martyr in the mid second century (*Dialogue with Trypho*, ch. 41).

It might seem that the scene was now set for the arrival of the 'four action shape', which is the theme of Gregory Dix's book *The Shape of the Liturgy*, and which has mesmerised most revisers of the liturgy since, including those responsible for Series 3. There has to be an offertory, a thanksgiving, a fraction and a distribution, in that order, if we are to conform to our Lord's institution, we are constantly told. Nothing, in fact, could be further from the truth. Our Lord's institution, as we have seen, was ninefold, not fourfold, and his interpretative words (the one original feature which he added to the meal, thus transforming it) are quite as important as any of the actions singled out by Dix. The offertory corresponds to none of the instituted acts: it is an act rather of the attendant than our Lord. Moreover, though the priest *receives* the elements at the offertory, this is in order to put them on the Lord's table, not in order to break bread and distribute. The truly functional taking of bread and wine which the priest performs, and which genuinely corresponds to our Lord's taking, is much later in the service. Nor are matters altered if the strange advice given in *The Presentation of the Eucharist* (p. 15) is followed, and the priest, immediately after putting the elements on the Lord's table at the offertory, takes them up again and puts them on it a second time before giving thanks. The claim that this conforms to the Passover liturgy cannot be substantiated, and it certainly conflicts with the institution narrative. Our Lord's taking of the elements from

55

the table (or from the attendant) was functional, with a view to distribution. Consequently, he took them singly, and proceeded with his purpose, in the same way as the priest takes them at the administration. He did not take them together, and put them down again, as it is proposed that the priest should do at the offertory. The acts of the traditional eucharist which correspond to our Lord's are therefore the giving of thanks, the recital of our Lord's words, the taking, breaking and distributing of the bread, the taking and distributing of the wine, in that order. It is a seven action shape, and significantly different from the four action shape detected by Dix.

The real origin of the offertory of bread and wine lies not in our Lord's taking of the bread and cup but in the fact that at a very early date in Christian history it became common for Christians to make their gifts for the work of God in kind, and to bring them to the Sunday service, where they would be publicly received and presented to God with prayer. Included among these gifts in kind, it was natural that people should bring bread and wine for the Sunday eucharist, but Hippolytus mentions oil, cheese and olives as things which people might also offer on this occasion (*Apostolic Tradition* 5. 1; 6. 1), and Sarapion, in the mid fourth century, mentions oils and waters that were offered at the service for use in healing and exorcism (*Sacramentary* 5f.). The offertory in kind was until the fourth century very widespread, and survived much longer in the West (see J. H. Srawley, *The Early History of the Liturgy*, pp. 47, 92f., 107, 123, 127, 136, 152, 168f., 193f.). And since the New Testament had described gifts to the ministry and gifts to the poor, even when made to them personally and privately, as sacrifices (Phil. 4. 18; Heb. 13. 16), it was natural that this language should be maintained when the gifts were brought publicly, liturgically and in kind, like the sacrifices of the Old Testament and of the pagan world. Hence, in the second century we find Justin Martyr (*Dialogue*, ch. 41) and Irenaeus (*Against Heresies* 4:17:5 to 4:18:6) speaking of the eucharist as a material sacrifice of bread and wine; and in the third century we find the *Didascalia* requiring that gifts for the ministry and the poor be brought to the bishop for him to distribute, and speaking of them as 'oblations which are offered through the bishops to the Lord God' (ch. 9). The language of offering was quickly extended from the people who supplied and brought the gifts, and thus 'offered' them (Hippolytus, *Apostolic Tradition* 5. 1; 6. 1; 20. 10), to the minister who received them and gave thanks over them: see *Apostolic Tradition* 5. 1; 26. 3, 6; 28. 2f., where 'to give thanks' over something and to 'offer' it seem to be interchangeable expressions. This, therefore, was the original meaning of Hippolytus's words when in his prayer of thanksgiving at the eucharist he represented the bishop as saying 'we offer unto thee this bread and this cup': it meant nothing more fearsome than does a prayer said today at the presentation of the alms. But it was only in its original context that this form of words could be properly understood. As soon as the offertory in kind began to decline, it was bound to be given a new meaning. And to revive such a phrase today, with or without an artificial offertory procession to support it, is simply an anachronism, which invites misunderstanding.

The presentation of the people's gifts in the *anamnesis* is the first item which Hippolytus's prayer adds to the institution. It may have been an appropriate addition when it was made, but it was always an addition. The second addition is the epiclesis, the petition that the Holy Spirit may come upon the elements and may unite and fill those who partake. The language of the early Church about the activity of the Holy Spirit in relation to the water of baptism or the bread and wine of the eucharist, suggests localisation, but when this is simply with a view to grace in the communicants, not a change in the elements, the notion has its edifying side, and can be turned to good purpose in present day worship by being reworded. All the same, it is unmistakably an optional addition to the instituted rite.

Passing on to fourth century liturgies, many differences are visible, the most striking of which are the appearance of the *Sanctus* as part of the giving of thanks, the use in the Roman liturgy of seasonal thanksgivings instead of a comprehensive one, and the general addition to the prayer of consecration of an extended intercession. Many, including A. H. Couratin,[3] hold that the last feature is due to the rise of the belief that the intercession should be made while the atoning sacrifice is lying on the altar (so Cyril of Jerusalem, *Mystagogical Catecheses* 5. 9). Others hold that this is a devotional interpretation of a change made for other reasons.[4] Certainly it is not a development without its doctrinal dangers, and it greatly lengthens the consecration prayer.

On these broad lines, the prayer of consecration now began to settle down. It was not until the Reformation that its pattern was seriously rethought. What changes did Cranmer make?

1. He prefaced the *Sanctus* with his confession, absolution and Comfortable Words, so that even when none of the Roman seasonal thanksgivings was appropriate, the *Sanctus* had specific reference to something—namely, to the atonement and the resultant forgiveness of sins. This had the further advantage of stressing the need for worthy participation, as required by 1 Cor. 11, to which Cranmer's exhortation at the beginning of the Communion proper makes reference. Series 2-3 has dealt with these issues in a different way, by restoring the comprehensive thanksgiving of Hippolytus and the Eastern liturgies, but retaining the confession, absolution and Comfortable Words. Cranmer's impressive link between the Comfortable Words and the *Sanctus* is not retained, however, so in the revision of Series 2-3 here published it has been optionally restored.

2. Cranmer stripped down the consecration prayer. The *anamnesis* with its words of oblation he removed, and located the words of oblation (revised so as to express the spiritual sacrifices of the New Testament) in his post-communion Prayer of Oblation. He also retained the language of oblation in reference to alms (another New Testament usage), confining it

in this case to the Antecommunion. He nowhere applied such language to the bread and wine, and he kept it out of the central part of the service. The intercessions he transferred to the old position, earlier in the service. He also made a separation between the *Sanctus* and the rest of the consecration prayer, which had never been closely united in the Roman liturgy, by the insertion of his Prayer of Humble Access. Thus, after being exalted to heaven in the *Sanctus*, the worshipper is humbled again in preparation for contemplating the cross and receiving the sacrament. This is the only communion devotion which Cranmer allowed to find a place within the sequence of the instituted acts. Series 2-3, with its longer consecration prayer incorporating the *Sanctus*, has had to find a different place for the Prayer of Humble Access. It has also introduced various communion devotions between the consecration prayer and the administration (a point at which Cranmer was particularly concerned to have no interruption of the instituted acts, because of the prevalence of adoration); and it has restored part of the Prayer of Oblation ('accept this our sacrifice of thanks and praise') to a place in the consecration prayer. In the revision of Series 2-3 here published, these two changes have been reversed.

3. For the Lord's Prayer, previously appended to the consecration prayer, Cranmer found an inspiring new position at the beginning of the post-communion. Series 2-3, which treats the Lord's Prayer as a communion devotion, has put it back more or less where Cranmer found it. This change also has been reversed in the revision of Series 2-3 which follows.

4. The remaining elements of the consecration prayer (the institution narrative and the petition for consecration to which, in the Roman liturgy, it was appended) Cranmer kept together, rewording the former so as to express a receptionist idea of consecration. In the address to God which introduced the petition, he strongly expressed the all-sufficiency of Christ's finished work of atonement at Calvary. Series 2-3 has blunted Cranmer's receptionism, and in our revision we have attempted

to sharpen it again, though rather in the Sharing of the Bread and Wine (paras. 31, 32) than here.

5. As regards the manual acts, the only ones explicitly referred to in Cranmer's 1552 Book are the distribution of the bread and the distribution of the wine. The taking of the bread and the taking of the cup are necessarily involved in these; and the fraction was probably intended to occur here also, as this was its traditional Western position, its natural, functional position, and its intended position in the 1549 service, to judge from Cranmer's language, which seems to imply that in 1549 it occurred some time after the institution narrative (*On the Lord's Supper*, Parker Society, p. 64). In 1662, a token taking and breaking were introduced into the institution narrative, and these have been retained in the revision of 1662 here published, as they are a much appreciated feature of the service and fulfil the function of visibility applying the institution narrative to *this* bread and *this* wine. The laying of the hand on the bread, and the same on the cup, have not been retained, however, as they can be mistaken for benedictions rather than designations, and also because, not being instituted, they have rather awkward positions, being immediately followed by the words 'Do this in remembrance of me'.

How, then, does Cranmer's rite relate to our Lord's institution? As a reproduction of the institution, can it stand comparison with Hippolytus or with Series 2-3? The answer is that it relates very closely, and can stand comparison well. For (if one disregards token takings and breakings in the institution narrative, such as are found in 1662 and Series 2, and concentrates on the functional acts) Hippolytus, 1662 and Series 2-3 *all contain the same seven instituted acts in the same order:* the giving of thanks, the recital of the dominical words, the taking, breaking and distributing of the bread, and the taking and distributing of the wine. What more need be said?

Perhaps just this: that if there is such basic identity of form, it may suggest a doubt whether there is really anything to learn from studying the history of the liturgy. A reader who is troubled by such a doubt should have a look at the background study to Series 2, *Re-Shaping the Liturgy*, by H. de Candole and A. H. Couratin. Though he may disagree with many of the views propounded, he will not be able to avoid seeing how profitable a thorough knowledge of liturgical history can be to men of reflective mind concerned to find the best way of constructing, expressing and performing a Communion service, out of all the ways that have in the past been tried. The drafter of Series 2 had learned much from the past, and anyone who attempts the less radical task of adapting 1662 must also be prepared to learn from the past. What he must not do, however, is to idolise the past, or any part of the past. One part must be related to another, and the whole must be seen in the light of the teaching of Scripture and the needs of the present day. The current temptation is to idolise the early patristic period—to treat it as an absolute norm, without being willing to test it by the New Testament or to admit that some of the things it contained were primitive in more senses than one! A discriminating study of primitive worship is certainly instructive. It shows the original character and meaning of much in worship that subsequently degenerated. But the fact must be faced that not everything then practised was ideal, that some things were capable of improvement and later were improved, that some things were bad and later were deservedly replaced, and that some things which were satisfactory then would not be satisfactory in the changed conditions of another age. No one has a higher regard for primitive worship than Canon Couratin—in some respects his regard for it is too high. Yet no one could have stated more clearly and firmly than he has done the imprudence of the sort of unqualified appeal to the primitive norm which was made at the 1958 Lambeth Conference. His words are these:

> The appeal to the Primitive Church, whether in doctrine or in liturgy, is always extremely dangerous. In liturgy the evidence is scanty, and subject to more than one interpretation. Doctrine was undeveloped, and there was much in primitive liturgy which

by later standards was theologically untrue. The ecclesiastical and social situation in the Church of the first three centuries was totally different from our own. Many of the liturgical practices of that period would be either meaningless or ridiculous today. By all means appeal to what is primitive. But don't limit your appeal in this way, for that is just archaeologising. You must always balance your appeal to the primitive with two other appeals, the appeal to what is theologically true, and the appeal to what is pastorally sensible.[5]

The Structure of the Liturgy

OUR discussion of the Evolution of the Liturgy has already involved us in considering many of the important points relating to the structure of the Communion proper. However, a few points relating to the Communion proper remain, and no attention has as yet been given to the Antecommunion. In addition, there is the question of the pattern of Sunday worship into which the service fits, since this has bearing upon its structure.

To take the last-mentioned question first: there is considerable difference of opinion among Christians as to whether the Lord's day is adequately sanctified by meeting for worship once. The New Testament gives no clear indication how many times the first Christians came together on that day, but if 'the Lord's day' means 'the day dedicated to the Lord', it is at least highly appropriate that Christians should come together on it for worship and mutual edification more than once. Certainly Cranmer intended people to come together more than once, for he carefully refrained from singling out any of the services as the 'main' service. He appointed a sermon only at Holy Communion, which indicates, as the Parish Communion movement rightly points out, that he intended everyone to be present for the first part of that service at least; but, on the other hand, he appointed baptism to be administered at Morning and Evening Prayer, 'when the most number of people may come together'. This might suggest that he expected people to come to church not twice but three times. In fact, however, he intended Morning Prayer, Litany and Holy Communion (or Antecommunion) to be said one after the other, with no pause between except for the ringing of a bell, as became customary in the reign of Elizabeth I and continued so down to about the beginning of this century. It is sometimes supposed, on the basis of the statements of certain seventeenth century writers, that this close sequence was not Cranmer's intention, but the *Reformatio Legum Ecclesiasticarum* makes his intention clear.[6]

If people can be expected to come to church more than once on a Sunday, there is not the same necessity for including every important aspect of worship in a single service. In the Prayer Book, the sermon at Holy Communion is expected to make up for the absence of one at Morning or Evening Prayer, and the confession and absolution, Old Testament lesson, psalms and canticles at Morning and Evening Prayer are expected to make up for the absence of anything of this kind in the Antecommunion. The aim of many clergy in the past to encourage Christians to be 'twicers' is not one that ought now to be lightly abandoned, whatever inroads the continental Sunday may make. All the same, the fact needs to be faced that many churchgoers do come only once on a Sunday, in some cases because their circumstances leave them no choice. And an additional consideration is that, even where a second service could be arranged, and people could attend it, it is not self-evident that a second formal service is the best way of using the opportunity of meeting. Group Bible study, or a service of a more spontaneous type, or a prayer meeting, would be a possible substitute. There is no real reason why everything of this kind should always be relegated to weekdays. The theological and psychological reasons for giving more scope to lay initiative in public worship apply to Sunday as well.[7]

The conclusion towards which these considerations seem to lead is that *each service should, as far as possible, include every important aspect of worship.* Carried to an extreme, this would necessitate having an administration of holy communion as part of every service, which would hardly be desirable. But the general trend of modern Prayer Book revision, according to which the Antecommunion incorporates leading features of Morning or Evening Prayer (the Old Testament lesson, psalms and canticles), just as Morning and Evening Prayer have by custom incorporated a leading feature of the Antecommunion (the sermon), seems wise. This edifying new reform has set a lead to the Church of Rome, and has taken one from the Antecommunion of the early Church, with its synagogue background.[8] The reform is especially necessary, now that Holy Communion is once more being commonly held at a main hour of Sunday worship. There is, however, one feature of Morning and Evening Prayer which the Antecommunion cannot so easily incorporate, the confession and absolution. This is because there are already a confession and absolution in the Communion proper. If these are moved forward to the beginning of the Antecommunion, as they have been in some recent revisions (the experimental Australian, New Zealand and Welsh revisions, for example), they lose their special connection with the reception of communion and the need for worthy participation, and become instead a penitential introduction to worship in general, for non-communicants as well as communicants. On the other hand, if they remain in the Communion proper, there is no confession or absolution for non-communicants. The solution seems to lie in making more use of the Ten Commandments. These are not a confession, but they at least give the worshipper an account of God's will for his life and the opportunity to respond with a plea for mercy; and various other ethical passages of Scripture can be used as alternatives on occasion (four are provided in the revision which follows). There is a strong move today to get rid of Cranmer's 'two penitential sections', not so much by omitting the Ten Commandments, as by putting them immediately before the confession, on the principle that 'through the Law comes the knowledge of sin' (Rom. 3. 20). But this ingenious move is open to objection on several grounds:

1. It seems to envisage self-examination by the Commandments, with a view to confession, in the course of the service itself. There is hardly time for this.

2. It wrongly assumes that Cranmer's 'two penitential sections' have a common purpose, and are kept apart arbitrarily. In fact, the Ten Commandments seem to have been included not so much for self-examination as for instruction in Christian living. The latter is certainly their purpose in Calvin's Strasbourg Liturgy (Cranmer's possible source at this point), since there they do not precede the confession and absolution but come after them.[9] Moreover, Cranmer made the Commandments a fixed part of the Antecommunion, to be used every Sunday, whether or not the Communion (with its confession and absolution) was to follow.

3. If, as in Series 3, the Decalogue is united with the confession and absolution not at the beginning of the Antecommunion but at the end, the special connection with the reception of communion remains somewhat obscure, while the function of penitential preparation for the service as a whole is frustrated. The section thus tends to appear an over-long penitential digression.

The 1662 and Series 2 arrangement seems preferable, therefore, and has been retained in the revision here published.

Another structural question that arises in the Antecommunion is *the relative position of the sermon and creed*. In the Eastern Church and in Spain, the creed is used at different points in the Communion proper, but in Rome it follows the sermon, at the end of the Antecommunion or between the Antecommunion and the Communion, being itself followed by the newly revived intercession and the offertory.[10] The Roman position is followed by the Church of South India and Series 2-3 and was recommended by the Lambeth '58 subcommittee on the Book of Common Prayer,[11] but Cranmer's position after the gospel also has points in its favour. One

65

consideration is that the uninterrupted sequence gospel-sermon-creed is awkward from a practical point of view. The only way to achieve it successfully is for the preacher to go to the pulpit before the gospel, and even at the end of it he needs a hymn (authorised in the Liturgy of the Church of South India and now in Series 3) to cover his descent, before the intercession begins. But the most important consideration is that not all sermons lead naturally into a confession of faith. A practical sermon, for example, leads more naturally into prayer. For these reasons, therefore, in the revision that follows, alternative orders for the sermon and creed are allowed, and a hymn is also allowed at the end of the creed. Such a hymn could be related either to what follows or to the creed itself: nearly 10% of the popular hymns in the hymn book are confessions of faith or expressions of trust in God.

If, in the Western liturgy, the creed hovers in the middle between the Antecommunion and the Communion proper, the same is true of the intercession over a much wider area of the Church. In the early liturgies, the Communion proper may be considered to begin either with *the expulsion of the unbaptised and other ineligible persons*, or with *the offertory of bread and wine*. The difficulty is that these did not take place together. The offertory of bread and wine customarily took place immediately before the consecration prayer, but the expulsion of non-communicants often took place earlier, before the intercession. This is the case with Hippolytus (*Apostolic Tradition* 22. 5f.; cp. also Justin Martyr, *First Apology*, ch. 65) and with a number of later witnesses, both Eastern and Western. The reason doubtless is that God has not promised to hear the prayers of non-Christians. However, when at the Reformation the expulsion of non-communicants was revived, and the intercession was again separated from the consecration prayer, Cranmer placed the expulsion after the intercession; and though in 1552 he had no offertory of bread and wine, it is clear that he regarded the intercession as belonging to the Antecommunion, since he included it in that part of the service which was to be read when there was no administration of the sacrament. If the 1662 revisers, when ordering the placing of the bread and wine on the Lord's table during the service, had likewise put this at the end of the intercession, all would have been clear, but instead they put it at the beginning, with the offertory of alms. They thus put it unmistakably in the Antecommunion, since the intercession was still appointed to be read when there was no administration, though the departure of non-communicants was no longer mentioned, owing to the disappearance of the medieval practice of non-communicating attendance at the sacrament. In locating the placing of the bread and wine upon the Lord's table with the offertory of alms, the 1662 revisers were following the Scottish revisers of 1637, and the motives of the latter were undoubtedly antiquarian, since they thought of the bread and wine as a material sacrifice, connected with the offertory in kind which existed in the early Church.

The beliefs responsible for this confusion are thus two: (a) that God has not promised to hear the prayers of non-Christians; (b) that the bread and wine for the sacrament are to be thought of as a material sacrifice. The first is certainly true, but it does not follow that non-Christians ought not to be present at such prayers: if they ought not, there is much else in the Antecommunion at which they ought not to be present. In fact, there is nothing in Scripture to prohibit their presence, and being present is quite likely to help them to faith. Cranmer was therefore right to ignore this consideration, and to put the departure of non-communicants after the intercession, at the end of the non-sacramental part of the service, and not sooner. With the resurgence of non-communicating attendance in the last hundred years, the suggestion that non-communicants withdraw at the same point as in 1552 has been restored in the Irish Prayer Book; and as the current movement to bring Holy Communion back to one of the main hours of Sunday worship seems to make the suggestion opportune in the Church of England as well, it has also been restored in the service printed below.[12]

The second belief mentioned, that the bread and wine are to be thought of as a material sacrifice, really derives, as we saw in the first section of this chapter (on 'The Evolution of the Liturgy'), from the large offertory in kind which existed in the early Church. Unlike the Scottish revisers of 1637, the 1662 revisers did not themselves speak of the bread and wine as a material sacrifice,[13] any more than Cranmer did in his 1549 Prayer Book; but the reason why the placing of the bread and wine upon the Lord's table and the offertory of alms were in all these Prayer Books put together seems likely to have been an awareness of the old offertory in kind or of medieval custom on offering days. The offertory in kind, however, had in the sixteenth and seventeenth centuries long ceased to exist, and, when taken out of this context, the presentation to God by the Church of a few shillingsworth of bread and wine, shortly to be received back again, does not warrant sacrificial language, since one of the principles of material sacrifice in the Bible is its costliness to the worshipper (2 Sam. 24. 24 etc.). What follows from this is not only that the sacrificial language of the 1637 Prayer Book about the bread and wine is better avoided, but that the placing of the bread and wine on the Lord's table is better kept separate from the offertory of alms. As Couratin puts it, when speaking of 'the Laying of the Supper Table',

> What will be needed in this section? A rubric naturally, ordering the placing of sufficient bread and wine upon the Table. . . . Certainly not an offering of money. Alms for the poor, and collections for church expenses, have no direct connection with the Laying of the Supper Table.[14]

The insistence of the drafters of Series 3 that the presentation of the alms must accompany the offertory of bread and wine, since it shares the same sacrificial character (*The Presentation of the Eucharist*, p. 14f), is thus quite at variance with the enlightened intentions of the drafter of Series 2.

But if the laying of the table is not to be combined with the offertory of alms, where is it to be placed? The most natural position is surely with the departure of non-communicants, where the Antecommunion ends and the Communion proper begins. The 1662 position, in the body of the Antecommunion, reminds non-communicants of what they are missing, but does not seem to serve any other good purpose; and now that the practice has died out of informing the minister beforehand of one's intention to partake, it may be impossible for him to know at this point how much bread and wine to put in the paten and chalice. The current tendency in revision is to locate the laying of the table much later, immediately before the consecration prayer, and this was encouraged by the Lambeth '58 subcommittee.[15] The reasons for locating it here are, first, to discourage the idea (which seems to have arisen in the minds of uninformed Anglo-Catholics) that there are two different sacrifices in the service—the offering of the bread and wine at the offertory, sometimes expressed by an offertory procession, and the offering of Christ in the consecration prayer; and secondly, to conform to ancient liturgical practice. Neither of these reasons has much weight. For Christ is not offered in the consecration prayer, and people must not be encouraged to think so; and the ancient practice of putting the laying of the table immediately before the consecration prayer occurs in sources which either do not mention the penitential preparation for communion, or put it in a place where it interrupts the sequence of the instituted acts, between the prayer of consecration and the distribution of the elements. But if the penitential preparation for communion is not to interrupt the instituted acts but is to come sooner, it still needs to come within the Communion proper, as we saw on p.64 ; and it will hardly be perceived to come within the Communion proper if it precedes the laying of the table. Experiment with Series 2 made this perfectly clear. There the division between the Antecommunion and the Communion proper was merely a paper division, consisting of two words of blue type, and was consequently often ignored or overlooked. The congregation would continue on their knees from the beginning of the intercession to the end of the peni-

69

tential preparation, and only then would the minister move to the Lord's table. The result was that the penitential preparation became effectively part of the Antecommunion, and lost all special reference to the reception of the sacrament. The Liturgical Commission, in preparing Series 3, has simply surrendered to this tendency, and included the penitential preparation in the Antecommunion, but in the revision here published the necessary rearrangement has been made, by beginning the Communion proper with the preparation of the bread and wine.

Passing on now to the consecration, it will be observed that in the revision of 1662 printed below there are *proper prefaces*, but not in the revision of Series 2-3. This is because the proper preface and the comprehensive fixed preface are two alternative methods of commemorating God's saving acts, the former method characterising the Western liturgy, from which 1662 developed, and the latter method characterising the Eastern liturgy. Both methods are old, but the latter is, to judge by the extant sources, older (going back, as it does, to Hippolytus), and because of this, as well as because of its impressive scope, it is popular with revisers of the liturgy and is adopted in Series 2-3. Series 2-3, however, retains proper prefaces as well, thus mingling the traditions and exposing itself to the charges of repetition and of needlessly lengthening a prayer which is already by English standards long. An additional danger which proper prefaces present in this context is that they will distract attention still further from that particular act of God which the sacrament is primarily instituted to commemorate, Christ's death. One can understand the Liturgical Commission hesitating to remove proper prefaces from Anglican worship altogether; and if more seasonal material than the collect and lessons is desired in Series 2-3, the seasonal sentences and blessings which Series 3 provides are possible ways of supplying it; but, as to proper prefaces, if there is to be a revision of 1662 as well as Series 2-3, there is no reason why proper prefaces should not be retained in the former, where they belong, and be omitted from the latter, where they are an intrusion. This, therefore, is the course that has been taken in the revision here published. In Series 2-3 Revised the proper prefaces have been omitted, but in 1662 Revised the proper prefaces have been retained. They have been kept to the same number as in 1662, since it was not thought desirable to introduce prefaces which were not Christo-logical, and so would distract from the basic theme of the sacrament. For the same reason, a hint of Christ's saving death has been introduced into each preface which did not have one already, and the Easter preface has been extended to Good Friday.

We pass on, finally, to *the structure of the post-communion*. In 1662, the section of the service after reception is long and impressive, while in Series 2-3 it is kept as short as possible. In the revision that follows, both lengths are allowed for, according to the occasion or the congregation's preference. The order of items has been slightly varied from 1662 and Series 2-3, so as to make the succession of themes more orderly, as follows: (i) praise and thanksgiving after reception, (ii) self-oblation, (iii) dismissal or benediction. This order also allows the doxology of the Lord's Prayer to lead straight into 'Glory to God in the highest', and allows 'Send us out into the world . . .' to lead straight into the dismissal. The *Gloria in Excelsis* is here printed in full, so as not to discourage its use in Cranmer's position, which was so admired by Gore and Frere, among others;[16] but a hymn has been allowed as an alternative, since there are about seventeen popular hymns of self-oblation or self-dedication in the hymn book, and the post-communion is the obvious place in which to use them. As to the Prayer of Oblation, not only that part of it which expresses self-offering has been retained in this responsive position, but the 'sacrifice of praise', which Series 2-3 (in the interests of doctrinal ambi-guity) removed from the prayer and put in the consecration prayer, has been brought back.[17] The most striking difference, however, between the post-communion of Series 2-3 and that of Series 2-3 Revised, is that the latter begins with the Lord's Prayer, like the post-communion of 1662. A tribute to Cranmer's position for the Lord's Prayer may be found in H. de Candole and A. H. Couratin's *Re-Shaping the Liturgy* (p. 32). The reasons why the drafter of Series 2, despite this tribute, and despite his express objection to interruptions between the instituted acts, moved the Lord's Prayer to come between the consecration prayer and communion, are that this is its oldest known position in the service (only fourth century, however), and that the words 'give us this day our daily bread' and 'forgive us our trespasses' are particularly appropriate just before reception.[18] Few people are likely to be convinced by arguments as insubstantial as these, and Cranmer's much loved position for the Lord's Prayer, which avoids opening the old gap between consecration and administration, seems definitely preferable.

The Language of the Liturgy

THE subject of liturgical language is much in people's minds. Indeed, it seems to be almost the only criterion by which some judge a revised service or declare it to be conservative or radical, regardless of its structure, meaning and doctrine. Unbalanced though this emphasis is, the fact remains that something which concerns worshippers so much cannot be an unimportant aspect of liturgy, and some basic principles on the issue urgently need to be established.

In Latimer Monograph 2, *Services of Baptism and Confirmation*, the following words were used:

> Liturgical language is a dignified, rhythmical form of language, designed for recitation, approximating to rhetoric and less closely to poetry. This means that good liturgical English will never be colloquial, and will tend to be literary in its vocabulary. It does not, however, mean that liturgical English need be difficult English, and still less is this so in an age when education is as universal as it is today.[19] Nor does it mean that there need be any flavour of the antique in it, which does not seem to be

essential to dignity, as is sometimes thought, and may on occasion even detract from it. We have therefore taken the Revised Standard Version as a rough model, though avoiding its occasional antiquarianisms; and like the Revised Standard Version we have retained the normal and hardly alterable vocabulary of biblical theology, and have continued to address God (but no one else) as 'thou'. In the last instance a change may be on its way, as the proposals for Prayer Book revision in Australia and New Zealand suggest, but we believe that the general principle on which we have worked is sound. However, it ought to be a recognised right of clergy in areas of less than average education to paraphrase words or expressions which they think will be unintelligible. Even an inadequate substitute for a word is better than the term itself, if it will not be understood at all (p. 21f.).

The change to the mode of addressing God as 'you' has now reached this country, with the publication of Series 3, and has been followed also in the revision here published. It is too soon, however, to say whether the change will prove generally acceptable (enquiry suggests that opinion is at present fairly evenly balanced), and care has therefore been taken to phrase our revision in a way which lends itself as readily as possible to translation back into the 'thou' mode. The 'thou' mode of address, through its disappearance from converse between men, has come to express the transcendence of God in a powerful way, and its retention in most modern translations of the Bible (including the Revised Standard Version and the New English Bible) means that there is an inconsistency between the text of a liturgy using the 'you' mode of address and the readings from Scripture which the liturgy includes. It may be that ultimately Christian opinion will go right over to the 'you' mode, and that translations of the Bible will be brought into conformity with it, but one cannot as yet be sure.

On the general question of the sort of language at which liturgy should aim, thoughtful comments from students of the English language seem to support the quotation above. Stella Brook, the author of *The Language of the Book of Common Prayer* (London, Deutsch, 1965), has written:

Liturgical language is primarily spoken language, but it is a highly formalised variety of spoken language. It is not just current, easy, vernacular usage. It involves an appraisal of the possibilities of spoken language. It has to take into account such homely but necessary considerations as ease of pronunciation, in speaking, intoning or singing; it has to take into account the ear's desire for good rhythmic balance; it has to take into account the aural satisfaction of rhyme and chime. It involves a heightening of customary speech forms and rhythms, not a levelling-down. Liturgical style has also to satisfy the silent reader, as well as the hearer, and this is a great demand to make on any language. For my own part, I think that only verse-drama stretches the resources of a language to the same extent. . . . I began by speaking of liturgical language as used to the glory of God, but of course it should also be used to the help of man. Now, I cannot think that man is significantly helped if the language of the liturgy becomes simply the language of the factory floor. The encounter with liturgical language should be an enrichment of experience, not a repetition of the ordinariness of everyday life (in *Liturgical Reform: Some Basic Principles*, London, CIO, 1966, pp. 15-18).

Similarly, Ian Robinson, after quoting from the 1662 Marriage service, writes:

We need such language for the serious occasions of life if they are to *be* serious. Especially, any explicit community, any common recognition of what matters in life, can only be expressed in a language of due seriousness ('Religious English', in *The Cambridge Quarterly*, vol. 2, no. 4, Autumn 1967, p. 304).

Again, Lenore Harty, senior lecturer in English at Otago University, writes:

We will be *hindered* if the language is ugly, at loggerheads with what is going on, and, as one child put it, 'rude to God' ('The Language of the Liturgy', pt. 2, in *Church and People*, New Zealand, 4 October 1968).

As to the success of Cranmer and his modern revisers in achieving the sort of liturgical English desired, there is some difference of opinion. Cranmer has been charged with being too much influenced by Latin liturgical rhythms, but Dr. Brook defends him (*The Language of the Book of Common Prayer*,

p. 89f.). His English is generally admired—by C. S. Lewis, W. H. Auden, and Robert Speaight, to name but a few. Lenore Harty is quite certain that the New Zealand revision is not a linguistic success: quoting *The Language of the Book of Common Prayer*, p. 219, she writes:

> I don't mean that it is *impossible* to write a good liturgy—somewhere there must be someone with a knowledge of English and the way it works *and* with a sensitive ear and the ability to make words do what he wants them to do, but the Commission hasn't found this paragon. This is not surprising, because in the twentieth century we suffer from something that did not afflict the sixteenth, and that is a split between written and spoken styles; and this divorce has been detrimental to both. For when this happens 'written style readily deteriorates into a stylised and unnatural idiom. It tends to employ a vocabulary that has ceased to be a genuine part of living speech. Spoken style, on the other hand, readily deteriorates into a loose stringing together of half-formulated thoughts. It becomes slipshod, riddled with vogue catchwords, pitifully limited in vocabulary.' This splitting of the language into two is a terrible handicap to be working under when you are trying to write something to be spoken aloud in public, so the Commission can hardly be blamed for their failure ('The Language of the Liturgy', pt. 1, in *Church and People*, New Zealand, 20 September 1968).

Dr. Brook takes a rather more favourable view of the language used by the Liturgical Commission in this country (*The Language of the Book of Common Prayer*, pp. 217-19), but Ian Robinson damns it with faint praise:

> There has been no attempt to re-write the Book of Common Prayer in journalese, and the re-written parts do show a grasp of formal English not common at the present day. But compared with the 1662 book the revisions are flat, churchy and undramatic ('Religious English', p. 328).

Whether Series 3 has approached nearer to the ideal or fallen farther short of it is a matter on which the experts have yet to deliver their opinion. The revision published here is another attempt to reach the same goal.

There can be no doubt that the sort of liturgical language here envisaged is the sort that has been traditional in the

Christian Church, not only in English but in other languages. The rhetorical style of the early liturgies (even the concise Roman style) was from the beginning a dignified, rhythmical type of language, which centuries of use must have made even more formal and solemn. It is sometimes objected, however, that the liturgy should follow the style of the Bible, which it uses so much, and that the style of the New Testament was that of popular Hellenistic Greek. As a further argument, the view of Jeremias and others is quoted that 'abba', at the beginning of the Lord's Prayer, means 'Daddy'.[20] It may be questioned, however, whether any sort of justice is done to the biblical conception of fatherhood as the object of honour and obedience by the use of modern terms of affection like 'Daddy'. The pupils of the rabbis called their masters 'abba': did this mean 'Daddy'? And as to the general question of the style of the New Testament, modern opinion is swinging strongly away from the idea that New Testament language is colloquial Hellenistic Greek. In *The Cambridge History of the Bible*, the article on 'The Biblical Languages', by Matthew Black, follows Nigel Turner and others in maintaining that New Testament and Septuagint Greek is not colloquial Hellenistic Greek, but is a unique language, deeply marked by Semitic idiom, and having literary affinities as much as spoken ones.[21]

The items in the Communion service which are translated from other languages (notably the Collect for Purity, the Ten Commandments, our Lord's Summary, the *Gloria in Excelsis*, the Nicene Creed, the Comfortable Words, the *Sanctus*, the institution narrative and the Lord's Prayer) are carefully re-translated from the original text or texts in the revision which follows. The translations of the *Gloria in Excelsis*, the Nicene Creed, the *Sanctus* and the Lord's Prayer which have been drawn up by an ecumenical body called the International Consultation on English Texts, and are adopted from the ICET publication *Prayers we have in Common* (London, Chapman, 1970) in Series 3, have not been adopted here. The ICET translation of the *Sanctus* is in our opinion inferior to

Cranmer's well-established translation, and the following objections may be brought against the other three texts:

1. *Residual antiquarianisms.* In the Nicene Creed, 'begotten of' is used for 'begotten by', 'kingdom' in the sense of 'reign', and 'world' in the sense of 'age'; in the Lord's Prayer, 'kingdom' is used twice, once in the sense of 'rule' and once in the sense of 'kingship', and 'deliver' in the sense of 'rescue'.

2. *Inaccuracies of translation.* In the *Gloria in Excelsis*, not only is the well-known inserted clause omitted, but several other clauses are omitted without warrant; in the Nicene Creed, 'has spoken' for 'spoke' disguises the historical completeness of revelation, and the paraphrase of the statement about the incarnation confuses our Lord's conception with his birth.

3. *Faults of style.* The opening few lines of the *Gloria in Excelsis* have the rhythm of 'pop' worship. The closing lines string phrases together in a lame and clumsy way. In the Nicene Creed, the phrase 'One in Being with the Father' is misleadingly ambiguous.

A few verbal points in the revision here published may call for comment.

1. In the invitation (1662 Revised, para. 21; Series 2-3 Revised, para. 31), the metaphorical sense of 'draw near' is brought out by the addition of the words 'to God'. The words 'draw near' are often misunderstood in a literal sense, owing to the fact that the direction in the rubric before the third exhortation 'the communicants being conveniently placed for the receiving of the holy sacrament' is no longer widely observed, and an explanatory addition seems therefore to be called for.

2. Also in the invitation (1662 Revised, para. 21), the words 'take this holy sacrament to comfort you' are used. Similarly, the first exhortation in the Appendix speaks of 'this most comforting sacrament'. It is often supposed that 'comfort', as used here by Cranmer, means 'encourage(ment)' or 'strengthen(ing)', which it certainly could mean in sixteenth century usage, as in the case of the Holy Ghost 'the Comforter'. But

77

there are various indications that Cranmer is using the word in its other sense of 'console' or 'consolation' (the sense in which we use it today). Thus, in the first exhortation of the 1549 service he speaks of the communicant receiving 'comfort and consolation' through the sacrament. Again, in words which now occur in the first exhortation and have been in the Prayer Book since 1549, he speaks of the troubled conscience receiving 'comfort' (i.e. consolation) through absolution. This refers to an absolution before the service, but to the absolution in the service he appends the 'Comfortable Words', derived from Hermann's *Consultation*, where the term used is 'Trost' (usually meaning consolation). Elsewhere, Cranmer explains how the soul receives 'comfort' through the Lord's Supper when 'she seeth nothing but damnation for her offences by justice and accusation of the law, and this damnation is ever before her eyes'; 'in this great distress the soul being pressed with heaviness and sorrow, seeketh for some *comfort*', and receives it through the sacrament (*On the Lord's Supper*, Parker Society, pp. 38-44). Similarly, he writes that the Lord's Supper 'was ordained for this purpose, that every man, eating and drinking thereof, should remember that Christ died for him, and so should exercise his faith, and *comfort* himself by the remembrance of Christ's benefits, and so give unto Christ most hearty thanks, and give himself also clearly unto him. Wherefore the ordinance of Christ ought to be followed: the priest to minister the sacrament to the people, and they to use it to their *consolation*' (*op. cit.*, p. 352). It seems likely, therefore, that Cranmer thought of those who took part in his service as receiving consolation for their conscience after the confession of their sins, first through the words of the absolution and the Comfortable Words, and then through the sacramental symbols.[22]

3. The Comfortable Words themselves (1662 Revised, para. 24; Series 2-3 Revised, para. 25) have here been stripped of their familiar introductory formulae. This is because it is so doubtful whether St. John intends us to understand Jn. 3. 16 as part of Christ's discourse or as his own comment. One

small benefit that results is that a selection of the Comfortable Words can be used when desired, instead of all four.

4. In the Lord's Prayer (1662 Revised para. 30; Series 2-3 Revised, para. 34), the request 'Hallowed be thy name' has been modernised as 'May your name be sanctified'. This is not likely to make an immediate appeal to the worshipper, but long searching has made us despair of finding anything better. A verbal form is needed, because of the parallel with the following two requests, so the ICET rendering 'Holy be your name' is unsatisfactory; and 'sanctify', unlike 'hallow', is at least a verb still in use, and one which is linked with God's name in the English translation of Is. 29. 23 and Ezek. 36. 23.

Notes

1. See the *Mishnah* (*Pesahim*, ch. 10); *Didache*, chs. 9, 10.
2. In the early liturgies, it is not through the words of administration that this recital takes place, but through the institution narrative. The words of administration in Hippolytus (*Apostolic Tradition* 23. 5-11) are not derived from our Lord's interpretative words. In Sarapion and some other liturgies there is no indication that any words of administration are used. In the *Apostolic Constitutions* and some other liturgies the words of administration are simply a brief extract from the words in the institution narrative.
3. 'Thanksgiving and Thankoffering,' in *Studia Liturgica*, vol. 3, no. 1 (Summer 1964), p. 56f.; 'Liturgy', in *The Pelican Guide to Modern Theology*, ed. R. P. C. Hanson, vol. 2, p. 176f. See also J. H. Srawley, *The Early History of the Liturgy* (2nd ed., Cambridge, The University Press, 1949), pp. 203, 227-29.
4. This is the view of W. J. Grisbrooke. See his article 'Intercession at the Eucharist', pt. 2, in *Studia Liturgica*, vol. 5, no. 1 (Spring 1966).
5. *Lambeth and Liturgy* (London, Church Union, 1959), p. 5f. Compare also the words of the PECUSA Standing Liturgical Commission in *Prayer Book Studies* 17 (New York, Church Pension Fund, 1966), p. 10.
6. See the section 'De Divinis Officiis', cap. 1-12 (*The Reformation of the Ecclesiastical Laws*, ed. Edward Cardwell, Oxford, The

University Press, 1850, pp. 88-94). An English translation of the *Reformatio Legum Ecclesiasticarum* is due to be published by the Sutton Courtenay Press, of Appleford, in 1972.

7. Canon J. Stafford Wright has pointed out to the editors that it is very often a person's psychological make-up that leads him to decide against worshipping in the Church of England, and to choose a more 'Pentecostal' type of worship. The Church of England ought to make provision for people of all psychological types.

8. See J. H. Srawley, *The Early History of the Liturgy*, pp. 30f., 82, 90 etc.; C. W. Dugmore, *The Influence of the Synagogue upon the Divine Office* (2nd ed., London, Faith Press for Alcuin Club, 1964), chs. 5-7. The revival of the Old Testament lesson and of psalmody between the lessons first occurred in the Bombay Liturgy and the Liturgy of the Church of South India, and was endorsed by the subcommittee on the Book of Common Prayer at the 1958 Lambeth Conference (*The Lambeth Conference 1958*, p. 2.82). The revision of the Roman liturgy was introduced in 1969, as a result of the second Vatican Council. It revived the same two items, together with the intercession after the creed.

9. See W. D. Maxwell, *An Outline of Christian Worship* (London, OUP, 1936), pp. 113-15. Cranmer had close links with Strasbourg in the persons of Peter Martyr and Martin Bucer. F. E. Brightman suggests many other possible sources, but in most of these the Decalogue is likewise after or quite independent of the confession and absolution (*The English Rite*, London, Rivingtons, 1915, pp. cxlviii, clvi-viii, 1041f.; 'The History of the Book of Common Prayer down to 1662' in *Liturgy and Worship*, ed. W. K. Lowther Clarke and C. Harris, London, SPCK, 1932, p. 139). For the mistaken view about Cranmer's intention, see H. de Candole and A. H. Couratin, *Re-Shaping the Liturgy* (London, CIO, 1964), p. 14f. That Cranmer recognised the value of the Commandments for self-examination is undoubted, but he intended this use to be made of them in the days preceding the service, not during the service itself (see the first exhortation in 1662 and the second in 1552).

10. See H. de Candole and A. H. Couratin, *Re-Shaping the Liturgy*, p. 18.

11. See *The Lambeth Conference 1958*, p. 2.83.

12. See paragraph 19, and (for the objections to non-communicating attendance) the exhortation to the negligent in the Appendix. The restoration of a rubric suggesting the departure of non-

communicants was also proposed in *The Book of Common Prayer with Altered Rubrics* (London, Murray, 1880), submitted to Queen Victoria by the Convocations of the Church of England.

13. The classic study of the 1662 language and its meaning is John Dowden's essay 'What is the Meaning of "Our Alms and Oblations"?' in his *Further Studies in the Prayer Book* (London, Methuen, 1908), pp. 176-222. The essay also deals (on pp. 186-190) with medieval custom on offering days, referred to below. On this, see also D. B. Wayne, 'Behind Cranmer's Offertory Rubrics: the Offering of the People in the Mass before the Reformation', in the *Anglican Theological Review*, vol. 51, no. 2 (April 1969).

14. 'Revising the Eucharist,' in *The Liturgical Congress at Carmarthen*, p. 23. See also C. O. Buchanan, *Modern Anglican Liturgies 1958-1968*, pp. 11-14.

15. See *The Lambeth Conference 1958*, p. 2.81.

16. See R. C. D. Jasper, 'Gore on Liturgical Revision', in the *Church Quarterly Review*, vol. 166, no. 358 (January 1965), pp. 30, 35f.

17. For the Liturgical Commission's purpose in making this change, see p. 28f. above. Cranmer's position for the Prayer of Oblation, no less than his position for the *Gloria in Excelsis*, extorted the admiration of Gore (*The Body of Christ*, London, Murray, 1901, p. 284f.). Less unexpected advocacy of this position may be found in *The Fulness of Christ*, by S. F. Allison and others (London, SPCK, 1950), p. 32; C. F. D. Moule, *The Sacrifice of Christ* (London, Hodder and Stoughton, 1956), p. 57; R. T. Beckwith and C. O. Buchanan, ' "This Bread and This Cup": an Evangelical Rejoinder', in *Theology*, vol. 70, no. 564 (June 1967), p. 268. In L. E. H. Stephens-Hodge's *Evangelical Eucharist*, even the offertory of alms is located with the Prayer of Oblation.

18. For his objection and his reasons, see his article 'The Eucharist under Revision', in *Tell Wales*, p. 47f. See also *An Order for Holy Communion* (London, SPCK, 1966), p.x. Elsewhere, Couratin makes the damaging admission that those in the fourth century who wanted to say 'Give us this day our daily bread' at this point interpreted the petition as requiring daily communion ('Liturgy', in *The Pelican Guide to Modern Theology*, ed. R. P. C. Hanson, vol. 2, p. 156).

19. Poetry, such as psalms, canticles and hymns, is an exception, since poetry by common consent has its own vocabulary and word order. The attempt of Wordsworth to prove that this

ought not to be so has only convinced people still more thoroughly that it ought.

20. See Joachim Jeremias, *The Prayers of Jesus* (*Studies in Biblical Theology*, series 2, no. 6, London, SCM, 1967), pp. 95-98.

21. Matthew Black, 'The Biblical Languages', in *The Cambridge History of the Bible*, vol. 1, *From the Beginnings to Jerome*, ed. P. R. Ackroyd and C. F. Evans (Cambridge, The University Press, 1970).

22. For this interpretation, the editors are indebted to the Rev. R. J. Coates, one time lecturer in liturgy at Tyndale Hall, Bristol, and founder of the Latimer House Liturgy Group.

4 Revision Policy

‹◇›

FROM THE REVIEW of our historical circumstances in chapter one, and from the account of doctrinal and liturgical principles in chapters two and three, it is now possible to draw some broad practical conclusions, and to develop them a little.

Uniformity and Common Prayer

IT was noted in chapter one that, despite the liturgical chaos which has developed in the Church of England over the past century, the bishops have never abandoned the hope of a restoration of order and discipline. As early as the first decade of this century, they were looking to liturgical revision as a means to the desired end, but unfortunately they seem never to have appreciated the necessity of thrashing out the doctrinal questions which revision raises. Liturgical revision has been thought of in terms of limited concessions to various viewpoints, on the grounds that the varied complexion of modern Anglicanism demands it; but in the choice of the proposed concessions little thought has been given to the question of their doctrinal rightness or to the need for consistency between what is conceded and what is refused. When asked in 1927-28 why they were making doctrinal changes, the bishops simply denied that they were doing so, but in W. K. Lowther Clarke's opinion they would have been wiser to admit it.[1] If they had admitted it, they would have needed to go further and to assess and justify the changes. In doing so, they might have won over the opponents of their actions; alternatively, they might have had second thoughts themselves; but either way the result would have been beneficial to the Church, in helping people to see why a particular change was being made, or why it had been judged better not to make it.

The desire of the bishops for a return to order and discipline is shared by the House of Laity in the old Church Assembly and the new General Synod, who have the laity's proper concern to be allowed real corporate worship in which they can join (as Cranmer intended), and not to be at the mercy of the clergy. In the view of the House of Laity, variations which do not alter doctrine can properly be authorised for purposes of experiment, but such experiment must be kept within bounds, so that it will not make the existing chaos worse, but will prepare the way for a return to greater uniformity; and the services embodying the variations, even when authorised, must not be thrust on congregations by the clergy against the congregations' wishes. These safeguards are all written into the Alternative Services Measure, and were put there mainly as a result of the efforts of the House of Laity, who voted three times, against the opposition of the other Houses, for an exhaustive definition of lawful authority in worship.[2] Similar concerns have been expressed in Parliament from time to time, and assurances on the matter have been given by the present Primate, both there and in Convocation.[3]

The motives for seeking greater uniformity in the Church of England are thus two. On the one hand there is the concern for order and discipline, which goes right back to the various Acts of Uniformity and the principle laid down in Canon 30 of 1604 that things in themselves indifferent cease to be so when commanded by those in authority. This concern was vigorously expressed by the former chairman of the Liturgical Commission, Bishop Dunlop, at the Minneapolis Anglican Congress.[4] On the other hand there is the desire for common prayer, such as unites clergy and laity in a congregation and unites one congregation with another throughout the Church. The former motive tends to be disliked in certain quarters because of the rigid instruments of uniformity which were drawn up in the past by despotic governments.   Uniformity today needs to be far more flexible, so that services can be adapted to varying occasions and circumstances, and can embrace a greater variety of prescribed forms, which no longer create the problem for congregations that they would have done in an age of illiteracy.   Uniformity also needs to give some scope for free prayer, such as is provided in the intercession of Series 2-3; and this permission might need to be greatly extended if the Church of England united with one or more of the Free Churches.   Such modifications, however, would in no way abolish uniformity, since the variants and deviations would all be contained and authorised in the text of the liturgy which everyone would have in his hands.   Neither order and discipline nor common prayer would therefore be hindered.

The virtues of common prayer have been eloquently expounded by G. W. O. Addleshaw in chapter five of his book *The High Church Tradition: a Study in the Liturgical Thought of the Seventeenth Century*, and by J. I. Packer in his little work *Tomorrow's Worship* (London, Church Book Room Press, 1966). Liturgical common prayer both expresses and develops the unity of the congregation, and can be a bond of union over a much wider area (as the Prayer Book has been at times throughout England and throughout the Anglican Communion), because, being fixed in form, it concerns itself with general and permanent topics of worship.   Indeed, if the liturgy is left too much to local whim, even common prayer within the congregation becomes unstable and insecure.   Common prayer has an educative function: it implements the Pauline principle that corporate worship must edify.   And, this being so, it needs to be the expression of common doctrine.   Discussion of doctrine cannot, therefore, be neglected in the revision of common prayer, and when doctrinal discussion has got as far as it can, there must be a readiness to forego introducing doctrinal modifications on which agreement has proved unattainable.[5]

Common prayer is dependent not only on the text of the liturgy, but also on the actions and setting of worship. It is therefore a matter for profound thankfulness that the Liturgical Movement has achieved widespread agreement among Anglicans and others that Holy Communion should be reinstated at one of the main hours of Sunday worship, and that the service should be performed in a simple, intelligible and corporate manner, bringing priest and congregation together, and giving the congregation more to say and do. The Liturgical Movement has in these respects restored and extended the principles of the Reformation.

There is also widespread agreement today that worship should be concise. At the beginning of this century, when the sequence Morning Prayer-Litany-Holy Communion was still common, S. C. Lowry wrote an article on the question 'Our Sunday Services: are they too long?' (*The Churchman*, vol. 26, no. 77, May 1912). No one is in doubt as to the answer today. Redundancy, prolixity and repetition are all coming under the axe, and psychologists are advising the Church that attention must normally be expected to flag when a service has lasted more than an hour.[6] This again is relevant to common prayer, for without attention common prayer cannot exist.

Conservative Revision or Radical Revision?

IF common prayer and a measure of uniformity are proper aims, then it follows that the goal of liturgical revision is not unlimited experimentation but a new, agreed liturgy—a new Book of Common Prayer. This would be open to revision from time to time, as the Prayer Book was earlier open to revision, between 1549 and 1662; nevertheless, it could also resemble the old Prayer Book in having stability, through not being altered more often or more radically than was necessary. But what about today? How radical does revision now need to be,

86

particularly in the case of the Communion service? Many hold that it needs to be very radical indeed. The Series 2 revision was explicitly offered to the Church as 'a radical revision'.[7] The archbishops were stated to have requested this, and the vice-chairman of the Liturgical Commission revealed that they requested it because the Commission had asked them to![8] The reasons for the Commission's desire to be radical are explained by A. H. Couratin as follows:

> I say, draft a new rite, because that is how we conceive of our job. It is, of course, possible to tinker with the present service. The Church of England tried to do this in 1928. The Churches of the Anglican Communion have tried to do this, both before and after that ill-fated date, without any real success. And the reason is not far to seek. The rite of 1552 is a superb piece of liturgical composition, the finest flower of Reformation liturgy. Even after it had been tampered with by Queen Elizabeth I, and again by the Caroline divines, it retains much of its old complete-ness. As a rite it is unbreakable. In the end you have only one alternative. You can either restore it to its original form, as it left the hand of its author; or else you must scrap it. So let us lay aside the past, and let us try and make a clean start, in so far as this is psychologically possible.[9]

This makes the drafter's motives sufficiently clear. Modest revisions like those of 1559 and 1662 do not really affect the character of Cranmer's service. Extensive revisions like that of 1928, designed to imitate antiquity and alter doctrine, are really inconsistent with the genius of the rite. But since the drafter would not have been satisfied with a revision which was not extensive, he judged it better to set Cranmer's service aside.

In the preceding three chapters, we have seen the fallacy of the idea that Cranmer's service is unsatisfactory because he did not know enough about ancient Christian worship, or because he had a defective grasp of Catholic doctrine, or because he did not believe in consecration, or because the 'shape' of his rite is wrong. These are the main charges that have been laid at his door. Other smaller criticisms, which (if valid) can easily be met by small changes, will be considered in the next chapter. However, it is already possible to say that, if Cranmer's service is as excellent as Couratin believes, and is innocent of the main faults alleged, it does not deserve to be set aside, but should be brought up to date; and that the highest status which ought to be considered for any radical substitute, however excellent, is that of a permanent alternative. The 1662 Communion service is not, like the 1662 Baptism service, in need of many important changes in order to adapt it to the conditions of the twentieth century. The devotion of many Anglicans to this service has always been intense, and it remains so. In 1944, R. J. Cobb wrote that most Evangelicals would concede the need for Prayer Book revision and would co-operate in it 'so long as the Communion service remained untouched'.[10] R. R. Osborn, in his book *Holy Communion in the Church of England* (London, Lutterworth, 1949), entitled its three chapters 'Cranmer's Achievement', 'Does Cranmer's Work Need Substantial Revision?' and 'An Alternative to the Policy of Major Revision'. The view he took was that 'far more freedom comes to worshippers by interpreting his liturgy than by revising it' (p. 101). As recently as 1963, the vicar of Islington, in his presidential address to the Islington Conference, expressed the hope that the Alternative Services Measure would 'make provision for liturgical revision in those wide areas where there is general agreement', but added that 'it may well be wise, at this present juncture, to agree not to attempt to revise the Service of Holy Communion'. One of the reasons given for this last suggestion was the desirability of avoiding controversy, but the suggestion still implied that Evangelicals were perfectly willing to go on using 1662 unrevised. They were by no means alone in this. The instinctive lay reaction against the replacement of 1662 by Series 2 has extended through all schools of thought. Numerous letters have appeared in the *Church Times*, in diocesan journals, in parish magazine insets and in the secular press, as well as in specifically Evangelical periodicals. Articles from literary laymen have appeared in *Theology* and the *Daily Telegraph*

Magazine under such titles as 'The Destruction of Common Prayer: a Lay Protest' and 'Breach of Faith', calling the new service an 'insipid hotch-potch', 'verbally dead' and 'emotionally barren'. A writer in *The Spectator* has protested that, compared with the old service, the new one is 'dry as a board'. Numbers of theologians and liturgiologists of all schools of thought have publicly expressed varying degrees of aversion for Series 2 and a preference for 1662 (or Series 1): these include G. G. Willis, T. G. Jalland, J. R. Porter, G. R. Dunstan, H. E. W. Turner, J. I. Packer and A. M. Stibbs. And so one could go on. Such strength of reaction (and it has not, of course, all been unfavourable reaction) certainly bears witness to the impression that Series 2 has made. But is also bears witness to the hold that the work of Cranmer still has on the minds and affections of Anglicans.

'It hath been the wisdom of the Church of England,' says the Preface added to the Prayer Book by the 1662 revisers, 'ever since the first compiling of her public liturgy, to keep the mean between the two extremes, of too much stiffness in refusing, and of too much easiness in admitting any variation from it' (or, as we should say, 'in allowing any change in it'). This policy was not just an unthinking conservatism, but arose out of the essential character of liturgy, which is a fixed form of worship, mainly concerned with topics of universal and unchanging significance, and dealing with them not simply in the way which the individual minister thinks suitable, but in ways which the Church in many places and many ages has thought suitable. Because liturgy has these permanent and ageless characteristics, a good liturgy is not changed unnecessarily, and the congregation, which soon gets to know and love it, would not wish it to be. Indeed, as Cranmer himself noted, in the statement 'Of Ceremonies' and Article 34, unnecessary change is so far from meeting the desires of the congregation that it strikes against unity and concord and wounds the conscience of the weaker brother. All the same, a degree of revision is from time to time unavoidable. The language, experience and circumstances of a nation do not stand still. The alterations which were therefore deemed to be necessary in 1662 (as the Preface explains) were of four kinds: clearer instruction to the minister; modernisation of language; use of the most accurate translations of Scripture; and adaptation and supplementation to meet changed conditions. In the twentieth century, further alterations under the first head would hardly seem to be called for; but modernisation of language and the substitution of more accurate translations of passages of Scripture would again be appropriate; and adaptation to new circumstances could be made in a number of ways:

1. The mode of government in England has changed from an absolute monarchy to a constitutional monarchy. The New Testament bids us pray for rulers (1 Tim. 2. 1f.), and we ought to do it in realistic terms.

2. The Church is now more aware of its missionary responsibility than it was in the sixteenth and seventeenth centuries, partly because of the great missionary movement of the eighteenth and nineteenth centuries, and partly because of the drift away from the Church among Englishmen since the beginning of the twentieth century. This change of outlook should be reflected in the liturgy. In the way that the liturgy prays for the Church, it should recognise the Church's evangelistic responsibility; and it should pray for the world as well.[11]

3. The educational standard of clergy and laity alike has risen considerably since 1662, and has risen even more since the Book of Common Prayer was first drawn up in the previous century. Over the same period, knowledge of the Christian faith has probably declined, but all worshippers can now read the liturgy for themselves, and there is nothing like the dependence that there was on learning it by heart. Consequently, a great deal more variety and congregational participation could today be introduced into the Prayer Book, and specifically into the Communion service, without making it more difficult for the worshippers.

4. Holy Communion is now commonly celebrated on week-

days and at various times on Sundays, not simply at the main hour of Sunday morning worship. Since all can now read the liturgy for themselves, there is no reason why it should not be made more flexible and adaptable to these different occasions, by distinguishing between essential, less important and purely optional parts.

5. Compared with the twentieth century, the sixteenth and seventeenth centuries were leisurely ages. People worked long hours, but they did not rush; they took their time about everything. In the twentieth century we do things more quickly, but we find that, in consequence, concentrated attention cannot be maintained for so great a period. In any case, we have come to the conclusion that the services of the sixteenth and seventeenth centuries were somewhat excessively lengthy. If we are to abbreviate them, however, and at the same time to make them more comprehensive by including a greater number of items in a single service (e.g. an Old Testament lesson, a psalm and a canticle in Holy Communion), it will be essential to avoid all forms of repetition and to make the literary style more concise.

6. No human composition is perfect, and in the three centuries since the Prayer Book service was last revised, various reasonable suggestions for modification have been made (as well as plenty of misguided ones). Some of these suggestions have arisen simply from study of the book and experience in using it, while some have resulted from comparing it with other liturgies past and present, and asking whether (simply on grounds of edification, not antiquity) its provisions are invariably the best conceivable.

If, in accordance with the principles of the 1662 Preface, the 1662 service were now revised in these ways, it would not be changed beyond recognition, but it would be brought into the twentieth century. Then for the first time the comparison with a service newly composed in the twentieth century, such as Series 2-3, would be on equal terms, and people would be able to weigh up the advantages and disadvantages of each (as they are supposed to have been doing since experiment with Series 2 began in 1967) undistracted by extraneous considera- tions like the fact that the 1662 service has never been brought up to date. Moreover, congregations which desired moder- nisation, but did not desire to move right away from the old service to something else, would for the first time have provision made for them. On the other hand, the existence of such a revision of 1662 would not rule out a radical revision like Series 2-3, provided the latter were conservative in doctrine, and had the status simply of an alternative. Ideally, all this could be left to the Liturgical Commission. However, the Liturgical Commission has as yet shown no willingness to bring 1662 up to date, and little willingness to bring Series 2-3 into conformity with the doctrine of 1662. It has therefore fallen to private persons like those responsible for the present monograph to perform the two tasks in the Commission's place. How successfully the work has been done must be left for the reader to judge, but since the Commission has been unwilling to undertake the work itself, it would seem to be open to any who think these revisions successful to press for their authorisa- tion under the Alternative Services Measure, so that they can be judged in use as well as on paper.

Notes

1. *The Prayer Book of 1928 Reconsidered* (London, SPCK, 1943), p. 78.
2. See H. R. M. Craig, 'Lawful Authority and Prayer Book Revision', in *Towards a Modern Prayer Book*, ed. R. T. Beckwith. For other expressions of the layman's desire for common prayer, see C. S. Lewis, *Letters to Malcolm* (London, Bles, 1964), ch. 1; G. E. Duffield, 'Towards a Reintegrated National Church', in *All in Each Place*, ed. J. I. Packer (Marcham Manor Press, 1965), pp. 100-03.
3. See, for example, his words in the House of Lords at the passing of the Alternative Services Measure, 18 February 1965,

and his presidential address to the Convocation of Canterbury, 13 January 1970.

4. 'The Liturgical Life of the Anglican Communion in the Twentieth Century', in *Report of the Anglican Congress 1954*, pp. 84-87.

5. See R. T. Beckwith, *Prayer Book Revision and Anglican Unity*. Cp. also C. S. Lewis, *Letters to Malcolm*, p. 15.

6. For advice on the psychological aspect of the length of services, the editors are indebted to Canon J. Stafford Wright.

7. *An Order for Holy Communion* (London, SPCK, 1966), p. vii.

8. D. E. W. Harrison, 'The Problem of Liturgical Revision', in *The Liturgical Congress at Carmarthen*, p. 10.

9. 'The Eucharist under Revision,' in *Tell Wales*, p. 41f.

10. 'The Duty and Difficulty of Close Adherence to the Prayer Book,' in *The Churchman*, vol. 58, no. 4 (October 1944), p. 151.

11. See U. E. Simon, 'Unliturgical Remarks on Eucharistic Liturgy', in *Theology*, vol. 74, no. 611 (May 1971), p. 203f.

5 Introduction to the Draft Service

◇◇

The Revision of the 1662 Service

SPEAKING one day of a distinguished contemporary who had modernised the writings of an author of the previous century, Dr. Johnson remarked: 'An author's language, Sir, is a characteristical part of his composition, and it is also characteristical of the age in which he writes.   Besides, Sir, when the language is changed we are not sure that the sense is the same. No, Sir, I am sorry Lord Hailes has done this.'   A Church's liturgy, however, is not the property of its author and his age, in the way that other literature is.   It is the property of the Church of every generation, and is consequently not to be regarded primarily as an ageless work of art, but as an instrument of worship for the present day.   There are congregations today which are perfectly capable of coping with 1662 as it stands, and one would be sorry if they were deprived of it against their will.   At the same time, even they are accustomed to depart at certain points from the rubric or text in the interests of congregational participation or avoidance of duplication between Holy Communion and Morning or Evening Prayer; and it would probably be more consistent if they adapted the service to twentieth century conditions with greater thoroughness.   In the revision of 1662 which follows, a thorough adaptation to twentieth century conditions has been attempted, and though the general character of 1662 has been

94

respected, the revision is intended to make it just as up-to-date as Series 3 and its revision.

Updating of this kind is only possible because the 1662 service is basically sound. As may be seen by looking back over chapters two and three, the 1662 service expresses the biblical meaning of the eucharist in an exceptionally accurate and full-orbed way, reflects a true doctrine of consecration, employs a structure genuinely corresponding to our Lord's institution, and shows right instincts about liturgical language. The service well deserves the tributes extorted from unwilling admirers. It is indeed 'a superb piece of liturgical composition, the finest flower of Reformation liturgy'. The claims of superiority to 1662 made by the Liturgical Commission for its own service (*A Commentary on Holy Communion Series 3*, p. 6) cannot be substantiated.

Nevertheless, not all the many criticisms that have been directed at Cranmer's work, sometimes by those who are sympathetic towards it, are as ill-conceived as the ones rebutted in earlier chapters. The defects detected are not, indeed, fatal defects: far from it. But they do give scope for modification when the service is being revised. The attack which the Lambeth subcommittee levelled at the 'length and language' of the corporate expressions of penitence in the Prayer Book was certainly unbalanced, and could well have been corrected if the subcommittee had given more careful consideration to the CIPBC report *Principles of Prayer Book Revision* which lay before it.[1] The attack had an unfortunate influence on the confession and absolution of Series 2, which have had to be amended in Series 3. Yet there are some grounds for claiming that in 1662 the theme of penitence is 'too recurrent',[2] at any rate if it is not balanced by more *bold confidence* in access to God. Joy and wonder there certainly are in 1662—think how gloriously the *Sursum Corda* and *Sanctus* are made to take up the theme of the forgiveness of our sins through Christ's death, and how joyously, after reception, the post-communion responds with thanksgiving and praise. The presence of Christ is also vividly expressed in 1662, notably in the third exhortation, the first of the Comfortable Words, the *Sanctus*, the words of administration and the *Gloria in Excelsis*. But expressions of assurance do seem to be somewhat lacking, at any rate until the Lord's Prayer after communion. In the revision that follows, we have attempted to make good this lack by rephrasing the opening of the Prayer of Humble Access. This may seem a small change, but it comes at a most significant point; and to be able to say at this point not something negative but 'We *dare* to come to your table, holy Father' could make a marked difference in the psychological impression which the service creates.

Then again, some of the small criticisms that have been made of the structure of 1662 do seem to have weight, particularly the criticism of the point at which the Lord's table is laid. The notices are also a rather regrettable interruption between the creed and the sermon. Both of these positions are due to the 1662 revisers, incidentally, and not to Cranmer himself.

It is objected that there is too much continuous kneeling in the service. More freedom and variety of posture could very well be permitted.

It is also objected that the service is too individualistic. But this is due far more to the rather uncongregational way it has come to be celebrated than to the words of the service, which are simply at pains to express the eucharistic teaching of the New Testament, and to guard against formalism. The way in which the Reformers intended the service to be celebrated was highly congregational (with priest and people together, everyone present communicating, and everything visible, audible and in English), except that they gave the laity little to say.

If one adds these criticisms to the suggestions that were made in the previous chapter about ways of adapting Cranmer's service to the needs of today, and adds also the principle that it is desirable to eliminate needless and confusing divergences between the revision of the 1662 service and the revision of Series 2-3 in the wording of substantially identical material, one has a full explanation of the changes that have been made in preparing the first of these revisions. The main changes are the following:

1. The language has been modernised, by altering words and phrases that are no longer in use or have changed their meaning, and by simplifying the style.

2. Newly revised versions have been produced for all the translated items in the service, whether biblical or liturgical in origin.

3. The same wording has been used for all pieces of text which occur both in the revision of the 1662 service and in that of Series 2-3.

4. The whole Antecommunion of the two revisions has been made identical, by a combination of features of the Ante-communion which have hitherto been peculiar to 1662 or to Series 2-3. It thus incorporates an Old Testament lesson, psalms, hymns or a canticle, and a flexible intercession, from Series 2-3; offertory sentences and occasional exhortations, from 1662; and something of the order and emphasis of both sources. Consequently, the creed may (as appropriate) follow either the sermon or the gospel; the creed is not obligatory except at one of the main hours of Sunday worship; but on that occasion not only is the creed obligatory but also the Decalogue (or one of its alternatives).

5. The post-communion in the two revisions has been slightly rearranged, and has been made more uniform by starting it, in both cases, with the Lord's Prayer. The dismissal (in Series 2-3 Revised) is the only item in the post-communion which is peculiar to either revision. It follows from this that the distinctive character of the two revisions really lies in the central part of the service—the preparation for communion, the consecration and the administration. Here there are differences of arrangement, and also much significant material peculiar to the respective sources, though fulfilling broadly similar functions. This material is, in the case of 1662 Revised, the third exhortation, the invitation, the proper prefaces, the

consecration prayer and the manual acts in the institution narrative; and in the case of Series 2-3 Revised, the peace, the call to confession, the consecration prayer, the invitation to reception, the breaking of the bread and the shorter words of administration.

6. In the Antecommunion, as is implied in paragraph 4, provision has been made for the service to be used as a whole at one of the main hours of Sunday worship, but without the loss of the most distinctive features of Morning or Evening Prayer (Old Testament lesson, psalm and canticle).

7. More provision has been made for congregational participation (partly in the way that it is already practised without the authority of the rubrics), since 1662 tends otherwise to be something of a monologue. The abbreviation of the longer ministerial items should also help here.

8. Much other abbreviation has been made. The first of the two Lord's Prayers has been omitted; the Prayer for the Queen, which comes at an odd place and is hardly necessary in view of her position in the intercession, has been omitted; conciseness of language has been aimed at throughout, and in particular the exhortations have been reduced to a more usable length; allowance is made for the words of administration to be said to groups; and some parts of the service are made optional, or obligatory only at the main hours of Sunday worship. These abbreviations compensate for the additions noted in paragraph 6.

9. More flexibility and authorised variety have been introduced, partly in the way just indicated, by making some items optional, either on all occasions or on less important occasions; partly by providing alternatives to the Ten Commandments and alternative positions for the *Gloria in Excelsis* and the creed; and partly by allowing free prayer in the occasional parts of the intercession.

10. The rubrics have been reduced in number and length, and often in stringency, so that, taken together with the new Canons, they say all that is absolutely necessary for present

day worship, but not more. It has been judged (not too optimistically, one hopes) that the rubrics prohibiting celebration without a congregation are no longer needed.

11. Certain changes in Cranmer's provisions made by the 1662 revisers have been altered again or reversed. The notices, which interrupt the ministry of the word, have been moved; the preparation of the bread and wine has been separated from the collection and placed at the beginning of the Communion proper; the suggestion that non-communicants withdraw after the Antecommunion has been restored; and the directions about supplementary consecration have been omitted again, as a matter which can be left to the minister's discretion.

12. Finally, a few significant changes of wording have been made. The intercession has been extended in scope to include the world as well as the Church; it now mentions the Church's responsibility for evangelism; it speaks of the Queen as befits a constitutional, not an absolute, monarch;[3] the introductory formulae to the Comfortable Words (quite possibly misleading in the case of Jn. 3. 16) have been removed; and the beginning and end of the Prayer of Humble Access have been altered, so as to express assurance of faith in approaching God, and so as to avoid the idea, which Cranmer seems to have shared, that there is some special connection between the blood and the soul.[4]

The Revision of the Series 2-3 Service

LUKE MILBOURNE was sarcastically described by Pope as 'the fairest of critics' because, when censuring Dryden's translation of Virgil, he added his own translation for purposes of comparison. Though censure of Series 2-3 is not the editors' purpose, it is difficult for them not to sense a likeness between Milbourne's position and their own. Yet, in writing a monograph on this topic, it would be absurd to ignore the

Liturgical Commission's service, its qualities being such as they are and its use so widespread. We will therefore take the bull by the horns and speak our mind, pointing out as we do so that the service here published is a revision of 1662 as well as a revision of the Liturgical Commission's service, and is not intended as a rival to either, but rather as a contribution towards its future development.

Censure, we said, is not our purpose, and we will begin with praise. Among the merits of Series 2-3 are dignity, vigour, consciseness, flexibility, the provision for congregational participation, the ingenious provision for free prayer, the generally clear order of items, the introduction of elements of Morning and Evening Prayer into the Antecommunion, the prominence given to thanksgiving as one of the instituted acts, and the helpful layout of the material on the printed page. In all these points, later revisers of the liturgy are debtors to the Liturgical Commission, and are glad to learn from its work.

The radical policy on which the Commission has performed its task was discussed in chapter four, and was judged proper, provided Series 2-3 does not aspire to be more than an alternative. In the published text this radical policy is disguised by the presence of various items from 1662, some of which the Commission did not venture to omit, others of which were added, on an optional basis, at the request of members of Church Assembly.[5] If it is decided that 1662 is to be brought up to date, so that it does not pass out of use, and that Series 2-3 is never to be more than an alternative to it, it will be possible for such of the optional 1662 items in Series 2-3 as are not important for the doctrine of the service to be removed again, since they will have a permanent home in the revised 1662.

The debate on the language of Series 3 is only just beginning, and we do not intend to add more to it than the general principles set out in chapter three. As regards the structure of Series 3, we questioned in chapter three the inflexible position of the creed, the new position of the Decalogue, the position at which the bread and wine are prepared, the combination of a comprehensive thanksgiving and proper prefaces in a single service, and the position of the Lord's Prayer. These issues were fully discussed in chapter three (in the section on 'The Structure of the Liturgy'). Here one may simply note that the removal of the preparation of the bread and wine to the beginning of the Communion proper, in Series 2-3 Revised, has the incidental advantage of making possible in the service Cranmer's inspiring transition from the absolution and Comfortable Words to the *Sursum Corda* and *Sanctus*, which (to judge from comments in the Church press) many worshippers have missed in Series 2.[6] Additional points which deserve making here are that the offertory sentences have wholly disappeared from Series 2-3; that in Series 3, by a curious inversion, the Comfortable Words precede the confession instead of accompanying the absolution; and that the Liturgical Commission has carried rubrical flexibility to excess, even for a period of experiment, in that no directions remain regarding the audibility of the minister's words or the visibility of his actions, and that even at one of the main hours of Sunday worship the psalm and (for most of the year) the Decalogue are entirely optional.

The doctrinal character of Series 3 does not suggest that the Liturgical Commission has wholly freed itself from its old principle of deliberate ambiguity. The service is still rather weak in eschatology, it still contains a vague prayer for the dead (now obligatory) in its intercession and the 'sacrifice of praise' in its consecration prayer, it still omits the Black Rubric and includes the rubric on the treatment of the remains which lawyers have declared makes reservation legal. All these points have been discussed in chapter two (in the section on 'The Meaning of the Eucharist').

It would be churlish not to mention the improvements that have been made between Series 2 and Series 3. These are neither small nor few, and but for the appearance of Series 3 the above list of criticisms would be a good deal longer and more emphatic than it is. Nevertheless, the list is still considerable, and in the view of the editors fully justifies the preparation of the revision here published. It will also fully justify the General Synod, and local congregations, in giving Series 3 a very careful scrutiny before taking decisions about it. Whether *all* the changes made between Series 2 and Series 3 are improvements may reasonably be questioned. Some who admired Series 2 will undoubtedly regard Series 3 as Series 2 spoilt. The departure of A. H. Couratin and Stella Brook from the Commission since Series 2 appeared may help to account for this.

The important characteristics of the revision of Series 2-3 which follows are simply the changes that are made to meet the criticisms listed above. In addition, three doubtfully edifying options (the *Kyries*, the *Benedictus Qui Venit* and the *Agnus Dei*) have been omitted, though anyone who wishes to restore them in use is not prohibited from doing so. The relation between the revision of Series 2-3 and that of the 1662 service is explained in the previous section of this chapter.

It is hoped that Series 2-3 Revised will point the way forward towards a final text for the Liturgical Commission's service which Evangelicals could agree to have permanently authorised —which they could all use, and to which they could all give a doctrinal assent, without conscientious scruples. Some of the changes which Series 2-3 Revised proposes would perhaps be regretted by other schools of thought (though it remains to be seen whether this would still be so when the theological dialogue envisaged in chapters one and two has made more progress than it has as yet); and structural changes are often more debatable than pure matters of doctrine. Nonetheless, it has been our aim never to make Series 2-3 more difficult for other schools of thought than 1662 is, and it is our belief that 1662 will increasingly be seen to provide a biblical norm for worship which Anglicans do not disregard without serious loss.

Notes

1. See *The Lambeth Conference 1958*, p. 2.81; *Principles of Prayer Book Revision*, pp. 21-23. The CIPBC report considers the charge of 'humanistic optimism' made against several of the recent revisions of the Prayer Book in the Anglican Communion, and finds the charge to some extent justified.
2. See H. de Candole and A. H. Couratin, *Re-Shaping the Liturgy*, p. 22.
3. Since the intercession is now extended to cover the world as well as the Church, it is inevitable that prayer for the nations includes non-Christian nations, and that prayer for rulers includes non-Christian rulers. The Queen's relationship with the Church thus disappears from the intercession, and thought needs to be given to the question where else in a revised Prayer Book her status according to Article 37 can find proper liturgical expression.
4. In the 1548 Order of the Communion, Cranmer also gave expression to this idea in the words of administration. The idea is to be found in Augustine, and may be older. Its origin probably lies in the ambiguity of the Latin word *anima* and the Greek word *psyche* ('soul' or 'life'), for the blood is certainly connected with the life (Lev. 17. 11 etc.).
5. The account given by A. H. Couratin is as follows: 'In effect it (the Liturgical Commission) produced a new service altogether. . . . But, in order to obtain the support of the less radical, a good many features of the old service were introduced by way of alternatives, and the resulting draft, viewed as a liturgical document, was untidy in the extreme' ('Liturgy', in *The Pelican Guide to Modern Theology*, ed. R. P. C. Hanson, vol. 2, p. 238f.).
6. See, for example, the report of the liturgical consultations in the diocese of Rochester in the *Church of England Newspaper*, 21 March 1969, and the letter from J. E. D'Aeth in *Theology*, vol. 73, no. 600 (June 1970).

6 Text of the Draft Service

◇◇

HOLY COMMUNION OR THE LORD'S SUPPER

[The service is set out as a single order of Antecommunion followed by alternative orders of Communion. The indispensable parts of the service are marked ††. Parts which are obligatory only at the main hours of worship on Sundays and other holy days are marked †. Optional parts are left unmarked. The parts of the service which are to be said or sung by the congregation are printed in text size bold type.]

The arrangements in church and the conduct of the service should help the congregation to hear what is said, see what is done and participate fully. These considerations govern the placing of the Lord's table, the seating of the congregation, and the direction in which those leading the service face.

The Antecommunion

INTRODUCTION

   1. *Hymn or Psalm*

† 2. **Almighty God,**
     To you all hearts lie open,

All desires are known,
And nothing is hidden from you:
Breathe into our hearts your Holy Spirit
And cleanse our thoughts,
So that we may love you perfectly
And give you the praise rightfully yours.
Through Jesus Christ our Lord, Amen.

† 3. **EITHER** *the Ten Commandments, with responses*:
God said all these things.
I am the Lord your God: you must not have any gods
other than me.
**Lord, have mercy upon us, and help us to keep
this law** (*and so after each except the last*).

You must not form an image for yourself, like anything
in the heavens, on earth or in the seas; you must not
bow down to them, nor serve them.

You must not abuse the name of the Lord your God.

Remember to keep the sabbath day holy. You must
do all your work on the other six days, but the seventh
day is a sabbath to the Lord your God.

Honour your father and mother.

You must not commit murder.

You must not commit adultery.

You must not steal.

You must not give slanderous evidence against your
neighbour.

You must not covet.
**Lord, have mercy upon us, and write all these
laws in our hearts.**

OR *Our Lord's Summary of the Law, with response*:
Our Lord Jesus Christ said,

The great commandment in God's Law is: 'Listen, Israel! The Lord our God is the one Lord; and you must love the Lord your God with all your heart, soul, mind and strength.' This is the first and great commandment.

The next commandment is similar: 'You must love your neighbour as yourself.' There is no other commandment greater than these. The whole Law, and the Prophets also, depend on these two commandments.

Lord, have mercy upon us, and write these laws in our hearts.

Alternatively, the Beatitudes (Matt. 5. 3-12), the More Excellent Way (1 Cor. 12. 31b-13. 7) or the Works of the Flesh and the Fruit of the Spirit (Gal. 5. 16-24) may be read, with the response

Lord, have mercy upon us, and teach us to walk in your ways.

4. **Glory to God in the highest,**
   And peace on earth among men he favours.
   We praise you, bless you, worship and glorify you,
   We give you thanks because of your great glory,
   Lord God,
   King in heaven,
   God the Father almighty.

   Lord Jesus Christ, only Son of the Father,
   Lord God, Lamb of God,
   You take away the sin of the world:
   Have mercy upon us.
   You take away the sin of the world:
   Receive our prayer.
   You sit at the Father's right hand:
   Have mercy upon us.

   For you alone are the Holy One;
   You alone are the Lord;

You alone, O Jesus Christ,
Together with the Holy Spirit,
In the glory of God the Father,
Are the Most High.

†† 5. *Collect of the day*

THE MINISTRY OF THE WORD

6. *Old Testament reading*

† 7. *Psalm*

†† 8. *Old Testament reading (if not used at 6) or Epistle*

9. *Psalm, canticle or hymn*

††10. *Gospel. If acclamations are used, when the Gospel is announced all answer*
Glory to God our Father!
and when it concludes
Praise to Christ our Saviour!

†11. *Sermon (if not at 14)*

†12. **We believe in one God,**
The Father, the Almighty,
The Maker of heaven and earth,
The Maker of all things, whether seen or unseen.

We believe in one Lord,
Jesus Christ, God's only Son,
Begotten by the Father before all ages,
God from God, Light from Light, true God from
true God,
Begotten not made,
One in godhead with the Father.

Through him all things were made.
For us men and for our salvation he came down
from heaven;
He was made flesh through the Holy Spirit and
the Virgin Mary,
And he became man.
He was crucified for us under Pontius Pilate;
He suffered and was buried.
On the third day he rose from the dead
In fulfilment of the Scriptures,
He ascended into heaven
And sits at the Father's right hand.
He will come again in glory to judge the living
and the dead,
And his reign will have no end.

We believe in the Holy Spirit,
The Lord, the Giver of life.
He proceeds from the Father and the Son;*
Together with the Father and the Son he is wor-
shipped and glorified;
He spoke through the prophets.

We believe in one holy, catholic and apostolic
Church;
We acknowledge one baptism for the forgiveness
of sins;
And we expect the resurrection of the dead
And the life of the age to come. Amen.

13. *Hymn*

†14. *Sermon (if not at 11). A hymn may follow.*

---

* The words 'and the Son' are not an original part of the Creed,
though they express a biblical doctrine also taught in the Athanasian
Creed and Article 5.

THE PRAYERS OF THE CHURCH

††15. *The Prayers of the Church may be conducted by one person throughout, or there may be a different leader for each section. Individual petitions and thanksgivings may be invited from members of the congregation.*

Let us pray for God's Church and God's world.

Almighty God, you have graciously promised to hear the prayers of those who ask in faith. Grant that we, and all in every place who confess your name, may be guided by your word and united in truth and love. Make us bold to proclaim your salvation.
(*Particular requests and thanksgivings for the Church may be added. Silence.*
Lord, in your mercy **Hear our prayer.**)

Direct this nation and every nation towards peace and justice; guide our Queen and all who govern; reform society, and turn men from selfishness and greed.
(*Particular requests and thanksgivings for the nations may be added. Silence.*
Lord, in your mercy **Hear our prayer.**)

Save and comfort the suffering. Assure them of your constant love, which will not leave them alone in their distress.
(*Particular requests and thanksgivings for the suffering may be added. Silence.*
Lord, in your mercy **Hear our prayer.**)

Receive our thanks for those who have died in faith, for the example of their lives and for the peace in which they rest. Give us, with them, a share in your eternal kingdom.
(*Particular names may be mentioned. Silence.*)

Answer our requests, Father, and accept our thanks, through our Lord and Saviour Jesus Christ. **Amen.**

†16. *Collection (if not made at door on entry). This may be introduced by the reading of Matt. 6. 19, 20; Acts 20. 35; 2 Cor. 9. 6, 7; 1 Jn. 3. 17, or similar verses of Scripture. It may be accompanied with a hymn.*

†17. *Presentation of collection. Words from 1 Chron. 29. 11, 13, 14 may be used.*

18. *Notices and banns (if not read before service). On appropriate occasions, such as the Sundays immediately before Christmas, Easter and Whitsun, one of the exhortations printed in the appendix may be read.*

19. *Hymn (if not at 16). This is the occasion for adults who are not taking communion to leave.*

The Communion
First Text: 1662 Revised

THE PREPARATION FOR COMMUNION

††20. *The bread and wine are made ready on the Lord's table for the communicants.*

21. Brothers in Christ, we have no Saviour but Jesus, and how greatly he must love us, wretched sinners though we are. For, in order to raise us from darkness and death to everlasting life as God's adopted children, he humbled himself even to die on the cross. It was in remembrance of his death, and as a pledge of his love, that he instituted this holy sacrament, in which we may spiritually feed on his flesh and blood. But we may only venture to receive it, St. Paul warns us, after we

have examined ourselves. For these benefits are not ours unless we come in penitence and faith; if we come in any other way, we profane Christ's body and blood, and eat and drink God's judgment. Judge yourselves, therefore, so as not to be judged by the Lord; confess your sins to him; and give him thanks that Christ has died for sinners, and by shedding his precious blood has obtained for us the innumerable blessings of salvation.

You, then, who sincerely repent of your sins, love your neighbours and intend to lead a new life, following God's commandments: draw near to him by faith, and take this holy sacrament to comfort you, first making a humble confession of your sins.

††22. **Almighty God, Father in heaven,**
We confess with shame that we have sinned against you
In our thoughts and words and actions
And the things we have failed to do:
The guilt is ours, and we deserve your judgment.
Yet now that we sincerely repent, have mercy upon us;
For the sake of Christ your Son
Forgive us the sins of the past;
And grant that from today we may always serve and please you,
Living a new life to your glory.
Through Jesus Christ our Lord, Amen.

††23. God our Father, who has promised forgiveness of sins to all who turn to him in repentance and faith, have mercy upon you. May he pardon all your sins, free you from their power, strengthen you in all goodness, and keep you firm to the end; through Jesus Christ our Lord. **Amen.**

24. *One or more of these gospel sentences:*
Jesus said, 'Come to me, all who toil wearily and are heavily burdened, and I will give you rest' (Matt. 11. 28).

God so loved the world that he gave his only Son, that whoever believes in him should not perish but have eternal life (Jn. 3. 16).

Here is a trustworthy saying, which deserves full acceptance: Christ Jesus came into the world to save sinners (1 Tim. 1. 15).

If anyone sins, we have an advocate with the Father, Jesus Christ the righteous, and he is the propitiation for our sins (1 Jn. 2. 1, 2).

THE CONSECRATION OF THE BREAD AND WINE

††25. Lift up your hearts!
We lift them to the Lord.
Let us thank the Lord our God.
He is worthy to be praised.
You are indeed worthy to be praised. Always and everywhere we owe you praise and thanks, O Lord, holy Father, almighty and eternal God, through Jesus Christ, your only Son, our Lord.*

◇◇◇

* *On the following occasions the relevant proper preface is here inserted.*

On Christmas Day and the succeeding seven days: Whom you gave to be born as at this time for us. Through the power of the Holy Spirit he truly took human nature from the Virgin Mary his mother, but without sharing in sin, and so became the Lamb without blemish or spot who has washed us from the stains of our sin.

On Good Friday, Easter Eve, Easter Day and the succeeding seven days: But we chiefly owe you praise for his saving death and glorious resurrection. For he is the true Passover Lamb, who was offered for us and has taken away the sin of the world. By his death he has destroyed death, and by his rising to life again he has restored to us life everlasting.

On Ascension Day and the succeeding seven days: Who after his resurrection clearly appeared to all his apostles, and in their sight ascended into heaven, to prepare a place for those he died to save; so that where he is, we also might ascend, and share his glorious reign.

On Whitsunday and the succeeding six days: According to whose true promise, the Holy Spirit came down as at this time from heaven, with the sound of a rushing wind and the appearance of tongues of fire. He rested upon the apostles, to lead them into all truth, and to give them zeal and boldness to preach to every people the good news of salvation; by which we have been brought out of darkness into the true knowledge of you and of your Son Jesus Christ.

On Trinity Sunday: For you and your Son and your Spirit are three persons and one God. What we believe about the glory of the Father, we also believe about the glory of the Spirit; and what we believe about the glory of the Spirit, we also believe, without difference or inequality, about the glory of our Saviour, Jesus Christ the Son.

Through him, therefore, we acknowledge the greatness of your glory; and with the angels, the archangels and all the company of heaven, we say without ceasing

Holy, holy, holy, Lord God of hosts,
Heaven and earth are full of your glory:
Glory be to you, O Lord most high! Amen.

26. **We dare to come to your table, holy Father,**
Only because of your unfailing mercy;
We do not deserve even the fallen crumbs.
But you are always the same:
To be merciful is your nature.
Feed us therefore on Christ,
That through eating his body and drinking his blood
We may be cleansed in body and soul
And be one with him for ever. Amen.

Or a hymn

††27. Almighty God, our heavenly Father, who in your

tender mercy gave your only Son Jesus Christ to suffer death upon the cross for our redemption; who made there a complete satisfaction for the sins of the whole world, offering once for all his one sacrifice of himself; and instituted this sacrament to commemorate his death, with the command that we should observe it until his return: hear us, merciful Father, and grant that we, receiving this bread and wine which you have made, in accordance with your Son's institution and in remembrance of his death, may all share his holy body and blood. For, on the night of his betrayal, he took bread [*The minister takes the bread*]; when he had given you thanks, he broke it [*The minister breaks the bread*]; and he gave it to his disciples with the words 'Take, eat; this is my body, which is now to be given for you.   Do this in commemoration of me.'   So too, after supper, he took the cup [*The minister takes the cup*]; and, when he had given you thanks, he gave it to them with the words 'Drink from this, all of you; for this is my blood of the new covenant, which is now to be shed for you and for many for the forgiveness of sins.   Do this, whenever you drink it, in commemoration of me.'   **Amen.**

THE SHARING OF THE BREAD AND WINE

††28. *The bread and wine are received by the ministers and distributed to the congregation with the words*
The body of our Lord Jesus Christ, which was given for you, preserve your body and soul to everlasting life. Take and eat this in remembrance that Christ died for you, and feed on him in your heart, by faith, with thanksgiving.
The blood of our Lord Jesus Christ, which was shed for you, preserve your body and soul to everlasting life. Drink this in remembrance that Christ's blood was shed for you, and be thankful.

††29. *Anything still remaining of the bread and wine which were*

*made ready on the Lord's table is consumed at a convenient
time before the ministers leave church.*

CONCLUSION

††30. **Our Father in heaven,**
May your name be sanctified,
Your rule established
And your will done,
On earth as it is in heaven.
Give us today our daily bread;
And forgive us the wrongs we have done,
As we too have forgiven those who wrong us;
And do not lead us into temptation,
But rescue us from the evil one.
For you are the King,
And the power and the glory are yours,
For ever.   Amen.

31. *'Glory to God in the highest' (if not used at 4) may follow, or
a hymn.*
Glory to God in the highest,
And peace on earth among men he favours.
We praise you, bless you, worship and glorify
you,
We give you thanks because of your great glory,
Lord God,
King in heaven,
God the Father almighty.

Lord Jesus Christ, only Son of the Father,
Lord God, Lamb of God,
You take away the sin of the world:
Have mercy upon us.
You take away the sin of the world:
Receive our prayer.
You sit at the Father's right hand:
Have mercy upon us.

For you alone are the Holy One;
You alone are the Lord;
You alone, O Jesus Christ,
Together with the Holy Spirit,
In the glory of God the Father,
Are the Most High.

32. Almighty and everliving God, we thank you for the spiritual food of our Saviour's body and blood. We thank you for this assurance of your favour, of our membership of his body the Church, and of our share in your everlasting kingdom. Keep us in his body, the fellowship of all who believe, and give us grace to do the good works you have planned. Through Jesus Christ our Lord, to whom be the glory, with the Father and the Spirit, both now and for ever. **Amen.**

33. **Almighty God,**
We offer you this service of praise and thanks-
giving;
We offer also ourselves, our souls and bodies,
To be a living sacrifice,
Through Jesus Christ our Lord.
Send us out into the world
In the power of your Spirit,
To live and work
To your praise and glory.   Amen.

††34. The peace of God, which passes all understanding, keep your hearts and minds in the knowledge and love of God, and of his Son, Jesus Christ our Lord; and may the blessing of God almighty, the Father, the Son and the Holy Spirit, be among you, and remain with you always. **Amen.**

The Communion

Second Text: Series 2-3 Revised

THE PREPARATION FOR COMMUNION

††20. *The bread and wine are made ready on the Lord's table for the communicants.*

21. We are the body of Christ. With one Spirit we were all baptised into one body. Those who gather at God's table must be at peace with one another. Do your utmost to maintain the unity of the Spirit in the bond of God's peace.
The peace of the Lord be with you.
And with you.

††22. Our High Priest is in heaven, Jesus the Son of God. He knows the weakness of our nature, for he was tempted in the same ways as we are. With complete trust in him, let us boldly approach our heavenly Father and make an honest confession of our sins.

††23. **Almighty God, Father in heaven,**
We confess with shame that we have sinned against you
In our thoughts and words and actions
And the things we have failed to do:
The guilt is ours, and we deserve your judgment.
Yet now that we sincerely repent, have mercy upon us;
For the sake of Christ your Son
Forgive us the sins of the past;
And grant that from today we may always serve and please you,
Living a new life to your glory.
Through Jesus Christ our Lord, Amen.

††24. God our Father, who has promised forgiveness of sins
to all who turn to him in repentance and faith, have
mercy upon you. May he pardon all your sins, free
you from their power, strengthen you in all goodness,
and keep you firm to the end; through Jesus Christ our
Lord. **Amen.**

25. *One or more of these gospel sentences:*
Jesus said, 'Come to me, all who toil wearily and are
heavily burdened, and I will give you rest' (Matt.
11. 28).
God so loved the world that he gave his only Son, that
whoever believes in him should not perish but have
eternal life (Jn. 3. 16).
Here is a trustworthy saying, which deserves full
acceptance: Christ Jesus came into the world to save
sinners (1 Tim. 1. 15).
If anyone sins, we have an advocate with the Father,
Jesus Christ the righteous, and he is the propitiation
for our sins (1 Jn. 2. 1, 2).

26. **We dare to come to your table, holy Father,**
Only because of your unfailing mercy;
We do not deserve even the fallen crumbs.
But you are always the same:
To be merciful is your nature.
Feed us therefore on Christ,
That through eating his body and drinking his
blood
We may be cleansed in body and soul
And be one with him for ever. Amen.

27. *Hymn*

118

THE THANKSGIVING

††28. Lift up your hearts!
We lift them to the Lord.

Let us thank the Lord our God.
He is worthy to be praised

You are indeed worthy to be praised. Always and everywhere we owe you praise and thanks, O Lord, holy Father, almighty and eternal God, through Jesus Christ, your only Son, our Lord;

Because through him you made all things in the beginning, and formed us men in your own image;

Through him you ransomed us from the slavery of sin, by giving him to be born as man and to die for us on the cross;

Through him you restored to us a living hope, when you raised him again in triumph, and exalted him to your throne above;

Through him you claimed us as your own people, when he received from you and poured upon us the promised Spirit of life;

Through him you will set us on your right hand, when at the end of this age he returns as King and Judge;

Through him, therefore, we acknowledge the greatness of your glory; and with the angels, the archangels and all the company of heaven, we say without ceasing
Holy, holy, holy, Lord God of hosts,
Heaven and earth are full of your glory:
Glory be to you, O Lord most high!

The cross revealed your glory, mighty Lord; there your Son defeated sin and death; and this commemoration of his cross displays your glory, until the heavenly feast at his return. Show us now your glory and fulfil his word, that the bread we here eat and the wine we here drink may be for us his crucified flesh and blood;

For, on the night of his betrayal, he took bread; when he had given you thanks, he broke it; and he gave it to his disciples with the words 'Take, eat; this is my body,

which is now to be given for you. Do this in commemoration of me.' So too, after supper, he took the
cup; and, when he had given you thanks, he gave it to
them with the words 'Drink from this, all of you; for
this is my blood of the new covenant, which is now to
be shed for you and for many for the forgiveness of sins.
Do this, whenever you drink it, in commemoration of
me.'

So, Lord, with this bread and this cup we commemorate
his all-sufficient sacrifice, offered once for all upon the
cross. We remember his resurrection and ascension.
We look forward to his glorious return. And we ask
you to accept our worship, and to grant that we who
eat and drink at your table may be filled with your
Spirit, and so bound to one another, through Jesus
Christ our Lord;
Through whom and with whom and in whom,
In the unity of the Holy Spirit,
All glory in earth and heaven, O Father almighty,
Be now and throughout all ages given to you.
Amen.

THE BREAKING OF THE BREAD

29. The cup of the blessing, which we bless,
Is it not a sharing of the blood of Christ?
The bread which we break,
Is it not a sharing of the body of Christ?
Because there is one bread, and we all share that bread,
We, although many, are one body.

††30. *The bread is broken into pieces.*

THE SHARING OF THE BREAD AND WINE

††31. *If the shorter words of administration are to be used, this*
invitation is read:
Draw near to God by faith, remembering that Christ
died for you; receive his body which was given for you

and his blood which was shed for you, and feed on him in your heart, by faith, with thanksgiving.

††32. *The bread and wine are received by the ministers and distributed to the congregation.* **Either** *with the words*
The body of Christ was given for you. **Amen.**
The blood of Christ was shed for you. **Amen.**
Or *with the words*
The body of our Lord Jesus Christ, which was given for you, preserve your body and soul to everlasting life. Take and eat this in remembrance that Christ died for you, and feed on him in your heart, by faith, with thanksgiving.
The blood of our Lord Jesus Christ, which was shed for you, preserve your body and soul to everlasting life. Drink this in remembrance that Christ's blood was shed for you, and be thankful.

††33. *Anything still remaining of the bread and wine which were made ready on the Lord's table is consumed at a convenient time before the ministers leave church.*

CONCLUSION

††34. **Our Father in heaven,**
May your name be sanctified,
Your rule established
And your will done,
On earth as it is in heaven.
Give us today our daily bread;
And forgive us the wrongs we have done,
As we too have forgiven those who wrong us;
And do not lead us into temptation,
But rescue us from the evil one.
For you are the King,
And the power and the glory are yours,
For ever. Amen.

35. *'Glory to God in the highest' (if not used at 4) may follow, or a hymn.*

Glory to God in the highest
And peace on earth among men he favours.
We praise you, bless you, worship and glorify you,
We give you thanks because of your great glory,
Lord God,
King in heaven,
God the Father almighty.

Lord Jesus Christ, only Son of the Father,
Lord God, Lamb of God,
You take away the sin of the world:
Have mercy upon us.
You take away the sin of the world:
Receive our prayer.
You sit at the Father's right hand:
Have mercy upon us.

For you alone are the Holy One;
You alone are the Lord;
You alone, O Jesus Christ,
Together with the Holy Spirit,
In the glory of God the Father,
Are the Most High.

36. Almighty and everliving God, we thank you for the spiritual food of our Saviour's body and blood. We thank you for this assurance of your favour, of our membership of his body the Church, and of our share in your everlasting kingdom. Keep us in his body, the fellowship of all who believe, and give us grace to do the good works you have planned. Through Jesus Christ our Lord, to whom be the glory, with the Father and the Spirit, both now and for ever. **Amen.**

37. **Almighty God,**
We offer you this service of praise and thanks-
giving.

We offer also ourselves, our souls and bodies,
To be a living sacrifice,
Through Jesus Christ our Lord.
Send us out into the world
In the power of your Spirit,
To live and work
To your praise and glory. **Amen.**

††38. *Either*
The Lord be with you.
The Lord bless you.
Go in peace.
Thanks be to God.
Or
The peace of God, which passes all understanding, keep
your hearts and minds in the knowledge and love of
God, and of his Son, Jesus Christ our Lord; and may
the blessing of God almighty, the Father, the Son and
the Holy Spirit, be among you, and remain with you
always. **Amen.**

39. *All depart.*

Appendix

*An exhortation of the following kind may be used at 18 when giving
notice of a coming administration of holy communion. It may, for
example, be used on the Sunday immediately before one of the great
festivals or on an occasion when the Antecommunion is being read by
itself.*

Brothers in Christ, holy communion will be administered, as
you have heard, on   . It is our duty to receive
it worthily, remembering with gratitude the goodness of our
heavenly Father in giving his Son both to die for us and to be
our spiritual food in this most comforting sacrament. Consider, therefore, the peril of daring to receive so holy a thing
unworthily, and prepare yourselves to come to this heavenly

feast in the spotless wedding robe which is required by God in Scripture.

The way to prepare yourselves is to examine your lives by the rule of God's commandments, and wherever you see that you have offended in will, word or action, to repent and confess your sin to God, resolving to mend your ways. And if you find that you have injured not only God but also your neighbour, you must ask his forgiveness as well, and make good, to the full extent of your ability, any loss that he has suffered at your hands. You must also be ready to forgive anyone who has injured you, otherwise you cannot expect God to forgive your offences. And you must certainly not receive holy communion without God's forgiveness, or you will simply add to the judgment under which you already stand. So, if you are a blasphemer or an enemy of the gospel, if you hate or envy anyone or are guilty of adultery or any other sin, repent, or stay away from the Lord's table. Remember what happened to Judas!

But since no one should come to the Lord's table without complete trust in God's mercy, if any of you cannot quieten his conscience by these means but is still troubled with scruples and doubts, he should go to a wise minister and unburden his mind, so that he may receive absolution and spiritual advice through the ministry of God's word.

An exhortation like the following may be used at 18 *when the minister sees the congregation neglecting to receive the sacrament.*

Brothers in Christ, holy communion will be administered, as you have heard, on   . Those of you who are duly instructed are all invited to be present, and I implore you, for our Lord Jesus Christ's sake, not to refuse. If a man had prepared a feast, and the invited guests were so ungrateful that without any reason they refused to come, he would rightly be indignant. Therefore take care not to provoke the indignation of God, who so lovingly invites you, by not being present at this holy supper. He will not think worldly concerns a good excuse. Those who refused the feast in the gospel because they had bought a field or cattle, or had got married, did not find their excuses accepted. And if you say, 'I am a great sinner and am afraid to come', why do you not repent and mend your ways? As you love your own salvation, I urge you to come. And when you come, receive. 'Drink from this, all of you,' said our Lord. 'We are one body, for we all share the one bread,' said St. Paul. To stand by without receiving is to mock Christ's ordinance. It is better to stay away than to do that. But if you stay away, consider from whom you are staying away: from the Son of God, who graciously laid down his life at the cross for your salvation, and commanded you to receive communion at his table in remembrance of his sacrifice; and from your brothers in Christ, who assemble there to feast on that heavenly food. Consider this, and by God's grace you will come to a better mind.

Any posture in which the sacrament is received should express humility, reverence and gratitude for the blessings which it brings to those who receive it worthily. It was for this reason that the Anglican Reformers maintained the practice of kneeling, although they repudiated any worship of the sacramental bread and wine or of a supposed physical presence of Christ's body and blood. For the sacramental bread and wine remain bread and wine, the worship of which would be idolatry; and the fact of Christ's ascension, in his humanity, excludes the presence here and now of his natural body and blood.

Index

DATE DUE

GAYLORD			PRINTED IN U.S.A.